William Jones, Robert Clayton

A Full Answer to the Essay on Spirit

William Jones, Robert Clayton

A Full Answer to the Essay on Spirit

ISBN/EAN: 9783744761758

Printed in Europe, USA, Canada, Australia, Japan

Cover: Foto ©ninafisch / pixelio.de

More available books at **www.hansebooks.com**

A FULL ANSWER

TO AN

ESSAY on SPIRIT.

WHEREIN

All the Author's Objections both *Scriptural* and *Philosophical*, to the Doctrine of the TRINITY; his Opinions relating to the *Uniformity* of the Church; his Criticisms upon the Athanasian and Nicene CREEDS, &c. are examined and confuted.

WITH

A Particular EXPLANATION of the *Hermetic*, *Pythagorean*, and *Platonic* TRINITIES.

AND

A PREFACE, giving some Account of an Author who published in *Defence* of the *Essay*.

By W. JONES, Rector of Pluckley in Kent, and Author of *the Catholic Doctrine of the Trinity*.

The Second Edition, improved and enlarged.

LONDON,
Printed for ROBINSON and ROBERTS, at No. 25, in Paternoster-Row; and M. FOLINGSBY, near Temple-Bar.
MDCCLXX.

ERRATA.

For Pages ix. x. &c. of the Preface, read i. ii. &c. P. xiv. of the Preface, line 5. for *synonimous* r. *synonymous*. P. xxiv. of the Preface, l. 24. for *indulgencies* r. *indulgences*.

Page 19. line 15. for *reference, to* r. *reference to*. P. 30. l. 17. for *respect, or other*, r. *respect or other*. P. 35. l. 6. for *Arius, his life*, r. *Arius's life*. P. 56. l. 13. for *scriptures, there* r. *scriptures there*. P. 64. l. 23. for *Churches, for* r. *Churches for*. P. 70. l. 24. for *concession, will* r. *concession will*. P. 80. l. 20, 21. for אהוה r. אהיה. P. 96. l. 6. for *plantisque, fœcundat* r. *plantisque fœcundat*. P. 99. l. 24. for *intelligencies* r. *intelligences*. P. 110. l. 8. for *Oanini* r. *Vanini*. P. 205. l. 23, 24. for *God, and king* r. *God and king*. P. 219. l. 25. for ηνεμονικον r. ηγεμονικον. P. 227. l. 12. for *effect* r. *affect*. P. 237. l. 12. for *did likewise* r. *it did likewise*.

PREFACE.

IT was not my intention to trouble or detain the reader with a preface; but some time after the following sheets were ready for the press, a pamphlet came forth with this title—*A defence of the Essay on Spirit; with remarks on the several pretended Answers; and which may serve as an antidote against all that shall ever appear against it.*—If the book itself should really be able to support such a Title-page, and be found answerable to the latter part of it, my labour can avail but little. I think, however, that I may be pretty secure of its making any impression to my disadvantage, as the author of it, in the first place, does not seem rightly to understand the very scope and design of the piece he has undertaken to *defend*.

He tells us, that the author of the *Essay*'s " *whole* book seems *only* intended, not to en- " force any explanations of his own, but to " shew how ineffectual all attempts to explain " this mystery (the doctrine of the Trinity) have " been hitherto[a]." Now, if he has enforced *no* expla-

[a] Defence, p. 5.

explanations of his own, then it would be impossible for me to extract and produce them: but the substance of them, in short, is as follows:—The person of the *Father*, only, is the *one supreme intelligent Agent:* the *Son*, and *Holy Spirit* are not really God, but *called so*, because by an authority communicated to them from the Supreme, they are commissioned to ACT AS GODS with regard to those inferior beings committed to their charge[b].—And so far is the *Essay*-writer from endeavouring to exclude *every* explanation, that his whole book is principally calculated for the support of *this*.

Let it also be considered, that in the *dedication* prefixed to his *Essay*, he hopes that " his " sentiments will by gentle degrees come, by " the blessing of God, to be made a part of " the established religion of the country[c]." If therefore, as it is asserted in the *Defence*, he has enforced *no* explanation of the Trinity; and it is nevertheless hoped in the *Essay*, that *his sentiments* will be made a part of the established religion; this is in effect to hope, that *Nothing* (by the blessing of God) will be established as a fundamental of the christian faith. So that this Gentleman, instead of *defending* the *Essay*, seems to have defeated its principal intention, misrepresented its author, and reduced his whole book to an absurdity.   Another

[b] See chap. V. of the following *Answer*.   [c] P. 51.

Another method of this writer, almost as hurtful to the cause he has undertaken as the former, is to assert what he cannot possibly know to be true, even supposing it were so, and what the world must know to be false. Upon the publication of the *Essay*, and to prevent in some measure (as the *Editor* expresses himself) the evil effects of that treatise, a justly celebrated discourse on the Trinity, by the late Dean *Swift*, was reprinted in *Ireland*. This discourse, the author now before us has assaulted with a great degree of prejudice and animosity; and after he has sifted some absurd and contradictory senses out of its expressions, and treated his lordship of *Orrery*, and other *able* and *learned* gentlemen, with great contempt for not having *skill enough* to make the same discovery, confidently affirms, that he has " shewn the *Dean* to have been *an Arian* in *his heart*[d]." Now, if the *Dean* has been so unhappy in his expressions, as to subscribe himself *an Arian* while he meant to declare himself *a Catholic*, he must surely have wanted common sense; a defect, which (in his day) he was farther from than most men living: if in his expressions he appears to be *orthodox*, and yet was, in the *secrets of his heart*, an *Arian*; this author must pretend to some degree of omniscience in being able to find it out.

[d] Page 32.

As a specimen of his comments upon the Holy Scripture, I may set down the evidence he has alledged in favour of angel-worship.

The *Arians* have always been greatly distressed to justify the adoration they allow to the second and third persons of the Blessed Trinity, while at the same time they place them in the class of created beings. It is therefore presumed in the *Essay*, that the worship of angels can be no idolatry, because it *terminates in the one only and true God:* to which a certain author[e] has very judiciously replied—" yet it seems, in St. *Paul's*
" style, being idolatrous, and *doing* (religious) *service to them which by nature are no Gods,* are synonymous expressions." But here, the author of the *Defence,* in order to avoid the conflict in which he seems apprehensive of a defeat, " cannot but lament the ill treatment the scriptures
" of truth meet with, when they light into in-
" discreet hands, who catch at a single verse,
" which without considering *the context,* they
" *wrest* to their own purposes: for in those words
" of St. *Paul,* the crime is, *serving them which*
" *are not Gods by nature,* without a commission
" from God for so doing; by which means,
" the service did not terminate in the one only
" and true God[f]."

That

[e] Of an article published in the *Dublin* Literary Journal for *December* 1751.   [f] Page 13.

That there are, in the world, men *unlearned* and *unstable*, who bend and accommodate the scriptures to some private purposes of their own, is a lamentable truth, which every serious Inquirer will be ready enough to confess: and the reader, I am sure, will agree with me, that the remark I have just now transcribed, is likely to afford us a most ample confirmation of it: for after this pathetic exclamation against ill treatment, indiscreet hands, and a disregard to the context, the verse itself contains an argument full and clear, and the disregarded context—*without a commission from God for so doing*—which gives a contrary turn, or, a *wrest* to the whole, is not St. *Paul*'s, but *his own*.

If the crime of the Heathens in worshipping their idols, consisted (according to this author's state of the case) only in a want of commission; then he must suppose it possible, for God to authorize that very crime, against which he hath pronounced the most extreme vengeance and malediction, the very *abomination that he hateth*[g]; for the adoration of the *creature*, to redound to the glory of the *Creator*; and for the worship of an idol, the stump of a tree, to *terminate in the one only and true God*.

I will in this place take the liberty of propounding the following short remark: that as it appears

[g] Deut. xii. 31. See chap. xxviii. 14, &c.

appears from the text of St. *Paul* above-cited, we are to worship those only who are (φυσει θεας) *Gods by nature*; and as all the primitive ecclesiastical writers, in their application of the term ουσια, *essence*, make it synonimous with φυσις, *nature*[h], it may, I humbly conceive, be inferred from hence, that the *Homoousian* doctrine, for the sake of which the *Arians* would reject both the *Athanasian* and *Nicene* creeds, is scriptural in its *term*, as well as in its *sense*. For, if we are to worship the *Son* and *Holy Spirit*, as the *Arians* themselves are forced to confess, they must be *God by* NATURE, ομοουσιοι, *of the same essence* or *nature* with God the Father*; if not, the adoration we pay to them must include us in that sentence of condemnation passed upon the idolatrous Gentiles. But to return to the author whose manner of reasoning I shall, in the next place, take some notice of.

Dean *Swift* tells us in his Sermon, that " about " three hundred years after Christ, there sprang " up an heresy of people called *Arians*, from " one *Arius* the leader of them: these (says he) " denied our Saviour to be God;" where the author immediately replies—" than which no-
" thing

---

[h] Ιςεον, οτι ουσια και φυσις ταυτον εςι παρα τοις πατρασιν. *Notandum est, essentiam & naturam idem esse apud Patres.* Leont. de Sect. p. 308.

* See the argument from the word φυσις farther insisted upon in the *Cath. Doctr.* p. 47. Edit. 3. 8vo.

" thing can be more false; for they did acknow-
" ledge him to be God[1]."

Here the reader should be informed, that this writer has *two* definitions of a God: by the first, there is a *supreme* and *true* God; by the second, a subordinate and nominal God, who only *acts as* such, of which sort he says there may be *three hundred*[k]. Now if it be said, that the *Arians* denied our Saviour to be *God*, he exclaims against the charge, as if it were false, when in reality nothing ever was more true. For Dr. *Swift* meant, and this author knew it very well, that the *Arians* denied *Christ* to be the *true* God; whereas he himself only means, that they did not deny him to be one of the *three hundred* above-mentioned.

Where he cannot disprove any thing, he puzzles and perplexes the whole cause, and by interweaving a proportionable quantity of falshood, renders a question, in every view of it, unintelligible; and so far he is certainly in the right; for error is not to be advanced either by truth or perspicuity. In pursuance of this plan, he confounds the *Consubstantialists* (that is, the *catholic Christians*) with the *Sabellians*, and the *Sabellians* with the *Consubstantialists*, in the following manner—" The *Consubstantialists* and the *Sabellians*
" (says he) agree *exactly* in their opinion of the
" indivisible unity of the substance of God be-
" tween the *three Persons* of the Trinity[1]."

Which

[1] Page 22. [k] Page 44. [1] Page 27, 28.

Which is impossible to be true: For if the *Sabellians* agreed so *exactly* in this matter with the *Catholics*, they must then have maintained that there *were* three Persons in the Trinity, between whom this indivisible union might subsist: but on the contrary, they affirmed the whole Godhead to be μια υποςασις, or μονοπροσωπος [m], *only* ONE *hypostasis or Person.*

Again: " When the Father, Son, and Holy
" Spirit," says he, " are declared by the *Atha-*
" *nasians* to be the same one undivided Person in
" reality; I own I do not see any difference be-
" tween that and the doctrine of *Sabellius*[n]."
First, he makes the *Sabellians* assert *three* Persons in the Godhead, who never allowed more than *one*; then, makes the *Athanasians* allow but *one* Person, who always asserted *three*; and then solemnly declares—that he sees no difference between their doctrines! This very precipitate gentleman ought to have reflected seriously on the notorious falsities advanced in his book, of which I could produce *many* more instances. If he should condescend to do this, at my earnest request, I would then recommend to him a comparison between *Rev.* ii. 2. and xxi. 8. being willing to hope, that those texts, when laid together and considered, may have such an influence upon his heart, as to induce him to alter

his

[m] See *Epiphan.* v. 2. p. 513.   [n] Page 42, 43.

his ſtyle, and favour us with a piece rather more chaſtiſed and correct, if ever he ſhould appear again in the capacity of an author.

I cannot obſerve in a more proper place, that he threatens the world with a treatiſe, whence it will " appear, that that part of our Eccleſiaſtical " Hiſtory, which relates to the diſpute between " the *Arians* and *Athanaſians*, is little better than " an heap of falſities and forgeries°:" For I apprehend that the forgeries above-mentioned will enable any reader to conceive a proper idea of an *Arian* turned *Hiſtorian:* If theſe are not ſufficient, let him attentively peruſe the author's whole book ; and if that will not do, let me beſeech him to conſider that account the moſt excellent and learned biſhop *Bull* has given of *Chriſtoph. Sandius*'s *Nucleus Hiſtoriæ Eccleſiaſticæ —copioſiſſimâ fabularum & contradictionum acceſſione locupletatus*—ᵖ and I am perſuaded he will then be upon his guard againſt every hiſtorical tract which comes from *that* quarter.

I ſhall now remark (and in truth I am almoſt tired of remarking) his raſhneſs in cenſuring what, it is plain, he has not properly conſidered. The celebrated and learned Dr. *Stebbing*, in a quotation this author has made from him, ſays,
" How

° Page 40.
ᵖ Def. Fid. Nic. Procem. § 6. See alſo *Pages* 69, 121, 229, & *alibi ſparſim.*—The *Irenicum Irenicorum* is another hiſtory of the ſame complexion with *Sandius.*

"How three, as diſtinct in point of *agency*, as "*Peter*, *James*, and *John*, ſhould by one com- "mon principle of exiſtence, be one eternal "God; this exceeds the meaſure of our finite "underſtandings to comprehend: yet it is not "therefore a contradiction; yet it is not there- "fore incredible." Which obſervation, though common, is yet very pious, well expreſſed, and worthy of a Chriſtian Divine. But, ſays our au- thor, " If the Doctor had but inſerted any one "noun-ſubſtantive after the adjective *three*, which "he, as all the *Athanaſians* carefully do, has "*diſingenuouſly* omitted, and without which the "whole ſentence is *nonſenſe**, he could not have "avoided ſeeing the contradiction, as well as "pointing it out to others ᵠ." The noun-ſubſtan- tive inſerted by the church upon this occaſion, is the word *Perſons*: and the moſt free and diſpaſ- ſionate enquirer can perceive no contradiction in ſaying, that the bleſſed Trinity are three *Perſons*, and one *God*; three and one, in *different reſpects*; three, in reſpect of their *perſonality*, and one in reſpect of their *divine nature*, or, as Dr. *Stebbing* has worded it, their *common principle of exiſtence*. To ſay, either that they are three Perſons and one Perſon, or, three Gods and one God, would
be

---

* He elſewhere ſays of this expreſſion, that it is—nonſenſe artfully cloathing itſelf, that it may look ſomething like ſenſe.   ᵠ P. 34, 35.

be to suppose them three and one, in one and the same respect, and would indeed amount to a contradiction in terms; which is the very thing this author has made of it: " for, adds he, " every one, who is not *out of his senses*, must see, " that affirming *three eternal Gods* to be *one eternal* " *God*, is a contradiction¹." Very true: and I hope no man that is *in his senses*, when writing upon such a subject as this, would dare to *make* a contradiction where he did not *find* one. But I must press this point a little farther: for it is observable, that the very same omission of the noun-substantive, and where the very same sense is expressed too, occurs more than once in the *inspired writings*, εγω και ο πατηρ EN εσμεν; and again, Ουτοι οι ΤΡΕΙΣ, EN εισι, *These* THREE *are* ONE—so that this bold accusation of *disingenuity*, *nonsense*, and something worse, alledged at first against Dr. *Stebbing*, will, when carried forwards, be at last fixed upon Him—whose name I dare not mention upon such an occasion.

In order to give a proper account of the *antidote*, and enable the reader, as well as I can, to comprehend the force and propriety of it, it will be requisite to premise a few of the author's principles, as they are to be collected from that part of his book, which precedes what is called in the Title-page—*An* antidote *against all that shall ever appear against* the Essay on Spirit.

The

¹ P. 34, 35.

The author of the *Defence* then, declares against all the *decrees of councils* and *doctrines of men*[s]; advises *metaphysical divines to forbear their own comments*[t]; and will suffer nothing but *clear and express revelation*[u] to determine *him* with regard to any article of moment. And yet, in express contradiction to all this, the ingredients of his *antidote*, which is to preclude all future controversies, to determine the question for ever on the *Arian* side, and (as its very name implies) to *expel* the poison of orthodoxy, are nothing more than a quotation from *Justin Martyr*[v], and another from the *Gentleman's Religion*[x]; the former a very obsure *metaphysical comment*, the latter a groundless and unsupported assertion. If we had not ocular demonstration for this, it would seem altogether incredible, that the same author who has rejected all *human comments*, and set at naught *all the councils in Christendom*[y], should think himself secure under the shelter of that very authority, nay, under a small and insignificant portion of it, the whole of which he has made it his business to vilify and contemn. Had he been more consistent with himself, and proposed his quotation from *Justin Martyr* with the sobriety that might have been expected, I should then have attempted to shew, that it contains *the indivisible union*

[s] P. 3.   [t] Ibid.   [u] P. 4, 50, 79.
[v] P. 54 to 78.   [x] P. 79 to 82.   [y] P. 29.

union of the Son with the substance of the Father; though blended, as I freely confess, with some perplexed and metaphysical reasonings, more reconcilable to the principles of *Plato*, than to those of the *Holy Scripture*. However, as he has introduced it in such a manner as to render it repugnant to his own principles, and therefore incapable of doing *his* cause the least service (be the doctrine of it this or that) I shall not try to give the reader any edification or amusement by a critical discussion of a very long passage, unlikely to afford either.

But I must not throw his book aside, without giving some short account of his language; I mean, of his candour, humility, and charity; which virtues are as much disregarded in the *Defence* (if that be possible) as they are recommended in the *Essay*.

The gentlemen who have advised the Reverend author of the *Essay* to resign his preferment; that is, in effect, to appease his conscience, retract his subscription, and cease to disturb the peace of the church with his own private scruples; he upbraids with a *spirit of persecution and ignorance*[z]: which is not more unkind than it is untrue and injudicious. For, on the contrary, those restless and discontented men, who have railed against the doctrines and authority of the church

[z] P. 52.

church as an intolerable burden, and have undertaken to supplant its truth by a surreptitious introduction of their own errors, (whatever specious appearances of candour and moderation they might at first assume in *proposing* them) have in fact, when affairs have taken an unhappy turn, themselves proved the most lawless persecutors and merciless oppressors of all *civil* and *religious* liberty: And I leave it to be considered, whether the spirit which has discovered itself in this *Defence*, were it permitted to have its full play, would not treat all its opponents with as little mercy as they did. Besides, how inconsistent is it, first to tell us that our doctrines and subscriptions are such as must *drive all men of sense and honesty* (such as the author is) *out of the church*[b]; and then, when we ground a slight admonition upon his own principle, to turn short upon us with the stale pretences of *popery! persecution!* St. *Dominic!* Bishop *Bonner! fire! faggot,* &c.[c]!

Dean *Swift* he calls a *Goliah* of *Gath,* sent out (by the republication of his sermon in *Ireland*) *to defy the armies of the living God*; and thinks he has *flung a few round pebbles of arguments so directly in his face, as to make him lie prostrate upon the ground*[d]. Which unnatural application of the Scripture-history gives us a taste of his vanity; and shews, that in his opinion the *Arians* are the elect

[b] P. 52. [c] *Ibid.* [d] P. 21. and 53.

elect people of God, the *true Israelites*, whilst all the opposers of their doctrine (which I hope includes every good christian in the nation) are uncircumcised *Philistines*, infidels, idolaters, and in professed rebellion against *the living God*.

The orthodox Clergy in general, he reviles as a set of cloudy, bigotted, indolent men, who, *if they can but preserve their subscriptions and good livings, care not what becomes of Christianity*[e]; because they have not wrote an answer (or had not at least when his book was published) to the late Lord *Bolingbroke*'s objections; and unless he *has written one himself*, it is unfair to make this a pretence for insulting *them*.

The learned gentlemen that have appeared in print against the *Essay*, he calls, *collectors of cavils*[f], *orthodox gentry*[g], men that *neither understand the dispute, nor any thing else*[h], *their own trumpeters*[i], *minor scribblers*[k], *animals*[l], *buzzing insects*[m], *hard heads*[n], &c. &c. charges the grave and learned Dr. *Stebbing* with wilful *nonsense*, the whole church with *blasphemy*[o]: then wipes his mouth, and humbly desires that if any body should undertake to *answer the Essay on Spirit*, they will do it with—*Christian* candour and moderation[p]!

From

[e] P. 52, 53. [f] P. 2. [g] P. 19. and 53.
[h] P. 15. [i] P. 17. [k] P. 51. [l] P. 52.
[m] P. 51. [n] P. 52. [o] P. 10, 44. [p] P. 52.

From this view of things, we cannot but conceive a proper opinion both of the talents and the *spirit* of this author; whom, in truth, it has given me much lefs pleafure to expofe, than concern that there was occafion for it. And now, if this *Defence* was written by the *author of the Effay*, what an amazing change of character is here! In the *Effay* it is—*Homo fum, humani nihil a me alienum puto* [q].—*That principle which directs us to ufe all men well, can never vindicate us in ufing any man ill* [r]—And again—*were it not that experience convinces us of the matter of fact*, it would be HARD TO BELIEVE *that mens paffions could carry them to that degree of animofity againft each other, on account of opinions* BARELY SPECULATIVE (fuch as the *Catholic doctrine of the Trinity* is fuppofed to be, and upon which the difpute has turned in *this Defence*) *which we find practifed in all countries, and almoft in all ages* [s]. There the ruling principle is an univerfal love and affection, making charitable allowances for every fect of men in the world; extending even to *Hereticks, Infidels, Jews,* and *Mahometans*; and lavifhly difpenfing, as from the papal chair, its indulgencies to every error under heaven. But *here* (in the *Defence*) a very different paffion is predominant; fo far from making allowances in favour of *error*, that it cannot bear even the leaft degree of oppofition from the

[q] Ded. p. 35.   [r] Ded. p. 35.   [s] Ibid. p. 33.

the sincere advocates of the *truth*; but vents itself in wilful forgeries, contempt, calumny, and all the overflowings of an enraged malevolence. The *Essay* and the *Defence* of it being generally allowed to have come from the same hand, the indecent heat and obloquy of this latter piece will oblige us to understand all the *candid expressions* in the former work as things uttered under a mask, and against the course of nature. Where the mind is misled, the spirit is very apt to be embittered: and *true charity* is the fruit only of *true religion*. Whence it comes to pass, that if gentleness and moderation are affected by the disturbers of our peace to serve a turn, they are pretty sure to appear in their proper character as soon as they are *contradicted*. When the wolf assumes the person of the sheep, the likeness is found only in the *skin*; the voice, and the teeth, and the claws, are just as different as they were before; and if the animal is suspected, and forced upon a scuffle in his own defence, the cloathing is of no farther service.

However this may be, it plainly appears, that the favourers of *Arianism* are not always candid and charitable: therefore I must beg leave to observe that if any learned gentleman, who is of their opinion, should think so inconsiderable a writer as I am worth his notice, and fairly propose his objections to any part of the following work with sense and argument, I shall be ready, with God's leave, to give him satisfaction to the best of my abilities, and with seriousness and moderation. But if any writer should unfortunately fix upon the same plan with the author of this *Defence*, and persuade himself that he can invalidate my arguments by setting me down for an *animal*, a *buzzing insect*, or an *hard head*, I can easily forgive him, but must be excused from making any reply.

When the first edition of this answer was published, it was heavily threatened, and I was assured that some sufficient hand would undertake to write against it: but nothing appeared, except some flourishes of the Bear-garden in a *Monthly Review*, the production of a set of writers, with whose principles, designs, and calumnies, the publick is now so well acquainted, that they will never think the worse of any *Christian*, because he is reviled and outraged in their publications.

If some may have been prevented either from reading or approving this work, or any other I have published, by the illiberal railings of *Reviews* and *News Papers*, the time may come when they will be undeceived: and if not, I have met with so much friendship and favour from men of genius, men of the best learning, and highest station, that I am already more than recompensed for all the detractions of infidelity, envy, ignorance or uncharitableness. The

The *Defence* of the *Essay on Spirit*, of which I have now been giving an account, is so empty of wit and argument, and withal so domineering in its manner and expression, that the reader may perhaps be discouraged from going through the following sheets, and think it scarcely worth his while to see the book itself confuted. Therefore I beg leave to assure him, that many articles of great importance are brought into consideration, to which I endeavoured as to do as much justice I was able: and there is among the rest a subject of great curiosity, the *Trinity of the Heathens*, which I have here opened as to its meaning, and illustrated it from prophane authors in a manner not to be met with in any other publication that I know of.

This answer was written at a time when I could not possibly have gone through it, under the disadvantage of my situation upon a country curacy, unless I had been favoured with the use of a well furnished library, belonging to my principal, Sir *John Dolben*, to whom the first edition was dedicated; a gentleman, whose memory I shall always regard with honour and gratitude, for the benevolence of his nature, his learning, and accomplishments, and above the rest his piety and charity: all of which were once so well known, and are now so well remembered, that it is not necessary for me to enlarge upon them in this place. When

When a man ventures to become an author early in life, it is very poffible that his zeal on fome occafions fhould be greater than his experience: and this confideration will, I hope, be of fome weight with thofe who are friends to the church, and are more than pretenders to learning, not to be extreme in remarking the imperfections of the following treatife; fome of which this latter impreffion has given me an opportunity of removing.

As to thofe readers, who are content to ground their belief (if I may call it fuch) on the infallibility of a *Clarke*, a *Sykes*, or an *Hoadley*, &c. I fhall be difappointed if I expect that they will either make any candid allowances for me, or venture to give me any of their arguments: and fo I leave them to proceed as they have hitherto done; not without befeeching God that he would open their eyes, and bring them back to the ways of truth, righteoufnefs, and peace, for his glory, and the faving of their own fouls.

Pluckley,
March 7, 1769.

A FULL ANSWER

TO AN

ESSAY on SPIRIT.

AN ANSWER TO AN ESSAY on SPIRIT.

THE author of this *essay* addresses his *dedication* to the Lord-primate of *Ireland*, and sets out with telling his Grace, that " as a clergyman, he
" was obliged to subscribe the articles of
" our religion, and give his assent to all
" things contained in the *Book of Common*
" *Prayer*; but since that time, having
" *thought*, as well as *read*, he finds that he
" does not now agree *exactly* in sentiment
" either with his *former opinions*, or with
" those persons who drew up the articles

" of our religion, or with the compilers
" of our Liturgy, and in particular with
" the *Athanasian* Creed; and therefore he
" has laboured under some difficulties
" how to direct himself in these circum-
" stances."

In all this the author gives notice to the primate, (and had his name been prefixed to the work, the notice had been very fair and honest) that he is at length become heterodox in his opinions. This he imputes to his *thinking* as well as reading. I am sorry to observe, that this change in his character is the reverse of what happened in St. *Paul*; who began first with *thinking*, and proceeded thence to *believing*. *I verily thought with myself* (saith he) *that I ought to do many things contrary to the name of Jesus of Nazareth. Acts* xxvi. 9. And though he appears to have been naturally a man of a tender and humane disposition, his mistaken way of *thinking* had so ill an influence upon his conduct, that he *beat in every Synagogue them that believed. Ibid.* xxii. 19. But when it pleased God to open his eyes, he was transformed from a
thinker

thinker into a *believer*; and consequently, from a *persecutor* into a *sufferer*; boasting of it as his privilege, that it was given to him *not only to believe* on the name of Christ, but also *to suffer for his sake*. The author will provoke us to consider this difference between *thinking* and *believing* in a more particular manner in the following pages.

As to the *difficulty* he complains of under his present circumstances, I apprehend it is no very difficult matter to direct himself properly on such an occasion; because nothing hinders him from resigning his preferments, if he objects to the conditions upon which they are held. He confesses, that he now differs in opinion from himself; from the persons who drew up our articles in conformity to the word of God; from those who in this age are subscribers to the faith; in short, he confesses that the whole established church is against him. Now he cannot surely be so unmerciful to our consciences, as to expect, that we shall disregard all these authorities; go contrary to the sense of the church in all ages; and calmly give up our faith and

and doctrine, in compliance with the opinion of one single person, who, not many years ago, was of a different opinion; and is perhaps but lately come to his present opinion: which is to suppose, that the truth of Christianity depends upon opinion; and that its very leading article, the doctrine of the Trinity, may be this or that, just as a wavering mind happens to *think*.

That vein of scepticism in which this author hath indulged himself, inclines him to *apprehend any attempt towards avoiding diversity of opinions, not only to be an useless, but also an impracticable scheme*. In the title prefixed to the Articles of the Church of England, the *avoiding diversity of opinion* appears to be only one half of the design with which they were drawn up; or rather, it is in fact the same thing with *the establishing of consent touching true religion*. If *true religion* then is of any importance to the world, the attempt to bring men to a *consent* about it is laudable, pious, and necessary. But if it matters not whether men embrace truth or falshood, whether they have the faith of Protestants, the superstition of Papists, or the

the herefy of *Arius, Socinus,* or the Alcoran; then the attempt to reconcile them to one and the fame rule of faith is, as this writer calls it, an *ufelefs fcheme.* If it fhould alfo be found *impracticable,* St. *Paul* hath publifhed an injunction which is very abfurd, becaufe no man can be bound to perform what is impoffible. *I befeech you brethren by the Name of our Lord Jefus Chrift, that ye all fpeak the fame thing, and that there be no divifions among you; but that ye be* perfectly *joined together in the* fame mind *and in the* fame judgment*. Such was the advice of this infpired Apoftle to the church of *Corinth:* But the author of an *Effay on Spirit,* having *thought as well as read,* hath difcovered that all attempts of this fort are *not only ufelefs but alfo impracticable.*

He is fond of this difcovery, and expreffes a doubt *whether any two thinking men are agreed exactly in their opinions.* If by *thinking men* he means learned chriftians, who have ftudied the Bible and primitive antiquity with a proper regard to both, I am very fure he is miftaken; for two fuch men,

---

* 1 Cor. i. 10.

men, if shut up in separate cells, as they report of the seventy Greek interpreters, would as surely agree in *sense* as they would differ in *expression*, if required to deliver their opinion concerning any fundamental doctrine of christianity. By *thinking men*, therefore, I suppose him to mean *deistical philosophers*, who think *at random*, or, as they call it, *freely*. If an assembly of these were to be questioned concerning their own inventions, there would probably be as many opinions as men, and all without foundation.

Thus much for the disagreements of *thinking men*; from whom the *author* makes a transition to what he calls, the *unthinking*, and observes, that *whatever country you go into, let the religion be what it will, the* unthinking part *are always the reputed orthodox*[c]. A truly christian account of the holy catholic church! which, it seems, is composed of nothing but men who *think* without *agreeing*; and men who *agree* without *thinking*. I would ask this gentleman, from whom the *unthinking herd*[d] of this

[c] P. 7.   [d] Ibid.

this nation derive the faith now eftablifhed in our creeds and articles? for if they did not alfo derive it from *another* unthinking herd, their orthodoxy will reflect no difgrace upon the religion of their *country*. But they derive it, thro' the miniftration of the Apoftles and their fucceffors, from *Chrift*; therefore the *herd*, whether thinking or unthinking, can as *orthodox*, be charged with nothing, but what, if carried far enough backwards, will equally hold good againft *Chrift* and his apoftles.

However we may boldly challenge him to *prove* the *orthodox* an *unthinking herd*; becaufe the men, who are the formal profeffors of orthodoxy, are thofe who folemnly fubfcribe their unfeigned affent to the orthodox faith, I mean, the clergy of the nation; who from the difcipline they undergo before they are called upon to give this proof of their orthodoxy, are fuppofed, at leaft, to be men of fome difcernment in matters of chriftian doctrine and human literature. Thefe then are the *unthinking herd*, thus reflected upon, of whom he charitably

charitably concludes, that if they submit to the Creeds, they do it without thought; for to think, in his sense, is to contradict the church. But neither will the subject bear to be inverted; for it is not altogether so clear, that ignorance will preserve an appearance of orthodoxy among the vulgar; rather the contrary. For most of those sectaries which have rejected orthodoxy, and look upon the glad and humble professors of it, as *Milton* represents the *Devil* to have looked upon *Gabriel**, have generally sprung from the root of ignorance; which, when nourished by a proper degree of pride, is always productive of error.

The *Quakers*, for example, arose from the ever memorable *George Fox*, a mean and ignorant mechanick, who could hardly spell his own name; yet, with bloody invectives against *Baal*'s *priests*, *execrable hirelings, devil-driven Judases*, with which,

and

---

* Proud *limitary* cherub! Par. lost, B. iv. 969. Had *Satan* been speaking to one of the orthodox, instead of *limitary*, he would have said, I suppose—*pacing in the trammels of the Church.* See *Middleton*'s Free Enquiry.

and many more such soft appellations he honoured all the true ministers of Christ, was enabled to draw away the *unlearned and unstable* into the very sink of error and delusion. Now, if *to think*, be to substitute heterodoxy, and a lying spirit in the place of sound faith and the spirit of truth, *George Fox* and his adherents ought to sit very high in the synagogue of *thinkers*; and if the author should still profess to *think*, in this sense, it may not be an unprofitable mortification to him, to see how much nearer the *thinking herd* approach to brutality, than those whom he is pleased to sneer for slavishly embracing the *creed of their fathers*.

He allows, indeed, that an *uniformity of profession may be both practicable and useful; and that it seems in some degree necessary— for the good of society* [f]. In this, if I am not so unhappy as to misunderstand him, he sinks the christian religion into a political scheme, calculated for the preservation of peace, or the *outward forms of society* [g], and intended only to make men hang together like

[f] Ibid.   [g] P. 9.

like a swarm of bees, which at the end of the summer, are to be smoaked out and buried in the earth. But the essential worth of the christian faith, is its great promise not only of this life, but of *that which is to come*. The good *of society*, without any thing farther, will sound very flat and dead in the ears of all those whose *hopes* are *full of immortality*; and is seldom recommended merely of itself, but by your little philosophical dabblers, who either disbelieve the resurrection, or do not expect to receive any advantage by it.

If an *uniformity of profession* be all that is necessary, and if even this be no farther necessary, than for the preservation of peace; then *any national religion*, established and agreed upon by compact and consent, would answer the end as well; since the external regulation of society would not, in this case, depend upon the *kind* or *quality* of the *religion*, but upon the *uniformity* with which it is *professed*. This sentiment, which favours strongly of infidelity, is nearly related to some others which I shall extract from the celebrated Dr. *Middleton*,

dleton, who in his angry letter to Dr. *Waterland*[h] has the following grave remark upon the *immorality* of *Tindal*'s scheme. "Should he then gain his end, and actually demolish *christianity*, what would be the consequence; what the fruit of his labours, but confusion and disorder, till some other *traditional religion* could be settled in its place; till we had *agreed* to recal either the *gods* of the *old world, Jupiter, Minerva, Venus,* &c. or with the *idolaters of the new*, to worship *sun, moon,* and *stars*; or instead of *Jesus*, take *Mahomet* or *Confucius*, for the *author of our faith?*" And to the same purpose, *p.* 55. "but should we consider it (*christianity*) as the *best of all other religions*, the best *contrived* to promote *publick peace* and the *good of society* — then his crime will be aggravated in proportion—since, as is said above, some *traditional religion* or other must take place, as necessary to *keep the world in order*."

I shall dismiss these sentiments with observing briefly, that a political agreement

in

[h] P. 51.

in the idolatrous republics of *Rome* and *Athens*, and peace and union under Chrift in the *houfhold of faith*, are things as different in their nature as in their value and importance; the former being wholly built upon temporal confiderations, and intended to prevent fellow fubjects from cutting one anothers throats; though the principles they went upon often made them do it, and were more frequently productive of anarchy, diforder, and bloodfhed, than of order, peace, and wholefome difcipline. The latter is grounded upon an *uniformity of faving faith*, revealed in mercy to loft mankind, by the righteous judge of all the earth, and implanted in the hearts of the meek and lowly; enabling them to bring forth thofe uniform and genuine fruits of love and charity to their fellow-redeemed, which will entitle them, as a nation, to the protection of God in this life, and at length exalt them to a place in the glorious affembly of the firft born, in the regions of everlafting blifs and immortality.

But it was his intereft to make an *uniformity*

formity of belief a matter so slight and trivial; or, if of any consequence, a *scheme* quite *impracticable*; and to recommend, instead of it, that *uniformity of profession* which would be no better than *deliberate hypocrisy*; that his readers might be the better prepared to receive his opinion concerning *subscriptions:* for as it is the design of his work to deny the consubstantiality and co-eternity of the ever-blessed Trinity, to which doctrines, as they now stand in our creeds and articles, he hath by a subscription declared his *unfeigned assent;* it must alarm the honest part of his readers, and put them upon enquiring, what method he has found of quieting his conscience? Why, truly, a very odd one; for it is his opinion, that *a man, for prudential reasons, may honestly subscribe and submit* to the use of *one established form, though he in his private opinion may think another to be better*[i]; and as for such of his brethren who differ from him, they *consider subscriptions in the same light with the bigotted members of the church of* Rome [k].

                                        Some

[i] P. 9.   [k] P. 17.

Some writers would be grievously at a loss, if they were not permitted to play the church of *Rome* upon us, when they have nothing else to say for themselves. The *articles* of the church of *England* are the best security we have against the errors of the church of *Rome*. When *Arianism* is let in upon us by the breaking down of our ecclesiastical fences, Popery may enter at the same breach : therefore the bigotted members of the church of *Rome* never yet were so blind to their own interest as to take part with those who are for keeping up the credit of our creeds and subscriptions: but, unless they are sorely belied, have co-operated against them in disguise with discontented parties of every denomination. He that considers this fact, will not be tempted to think lightly of moral honesty or christian fidelity, because a designing writer is pleased to stigmatise such parts of it with the name of popery, as really have nothing to do with popery; or if at all concerned with it, are directly against it. For if we are not *strictly bound* by a subscription to be Christians

tians and Protestants, we may subscribe with our hands, and declare with our lips, and yet in our hearts be very *Papists, Jews, Mahometans,* or what we please.

I must therefore ask, for what purpose any man subscribes to, what the author calls, an *established form,* that is, to the *book of common prayer,* and all the doctrines therein contained, but to satisfy the church that he *believes them?*

It hath often been insisted upon, and that with the utmost truth and propriety, that our articles are articles of *doctrine.* That kind of *assent* which is given to *christian doctrines,* we call *faith;* therefore, when a person declares his *assent* to these doctrines, we must of necessity understand that he *believes* them; or that the Church of *England* is so loose in its obligations, as to allow a man to declare one thing and mean another.

If such prevarications as these should be admitted, how can the state be secure of any man's fidelity, or the king of his allegiance, when the same subtilties which can explain away his ecclesiastical subscription,

C

tion, will prevent the moſt ſolemn ſtate oaths from binding him? This is ſuch a violation of truth and honeſty, as muſt give offence to every one who wiſhes well either to the church or ſtate; for ſhould ſuch looſe principles prevail, the moſt important contracts, nay (I repeat it again) the moſt ſolemn oaths, on whatſoever occaſion ſubmitted to, may be broken aſunder by thoſe who are reſolved to have the liberty of turning with every blaſt.

He may laugh, if he pleaſes, at ſome who *take occaſion, from the form of declaration of aſſent, to brand thoſe who preſume to doubt, or differ from them in any of their* IMAGINARY ORTHODOX *notions, with the imputation of perjury, or at leaſt of hypocriſy*[1]; for whoſoever ſets up theſe principles muſt be guilty of one or both; and though the author were maſter of as much ridicule as a late *Iriſh Dean*, any plain man, who will abide by his common ſenſe, might, upon this ſubject at leaſt, be an overmatch for him.

But

[1] P. 17.

But he has found out a remedy which he thinks sufficient, if not to remove these difficulties, yet to make him *pretty easy* [m] under them; if not to heal the wound, yet to stupify the part in such a manner, as to render it insensible: for though by the express words of the declaration, every clergyman is obliged to declare his *unfeigned assent, and consent to all and every thing contained and prescribed in, and by the book of common prayer*; yet since it is said in the *act of uniformity*, that he shall declare his assent, and consent *to the use of* all things contained in the said book, he may read the declaration with a *latent reference* [n], to the intention of the act, and thereby assent to nothing more than *the use of* the things, which, in the essay-writer's opinion, *is very different from assenting to the things themselves* [o].

Such *latent references* as take away the meaning of what a man declares plainly with his lips, would agree better with the character of a *Jesuit*, than that of a protestant Clergyman. However, the refe-

[m] P. 12. [n] P. 16. [o] P. 12.

rence here pleaded for is not reasonable; and if it were allowed, it would not come up to the author's purpose. It is not a reasonable reference, because it is much more natural, that the sense of the act should be gathered from the words of the declaration, than that the sense of the declaration should be explained by some preparatory expressions in the act; and to guard against this or any other evasion of the declaration, it is purposely enjoined that the declaration be made *in those words and no other*. This was then imagined to be a full and sufficient security, the church not being aware that any protestant would borrow from the papists the doctrine of *latent references*.

But even granting (which I have neither right nor reason to do) either that these words were transplanted from the act into the declaration; or that in the declaration he might be indulged with a *latent reference* to them, this would not answer the author's purpose. For in the book of Common Prayer, *to the use* of which he gives his assent, are there not *creeds* and
articles,

articles, as well as offices, prayers, and fuffrages? And how a *creed,* or an article of doctrine, can poffibly be *ufed* otherways than by being *believed,* I own, I am wholly unable to fee.

Befides, to fay nothing of creeds and articles, how can any perfon affent to the *ufe* of fuch *prayers* as exprefs fupreme adoration to the perfons of Chrift and the Holy Spirit, when he has perfuaded himfelf, and would perfuade others, that fuch worfhip is *idolatrous?* It is prefumed, what is here faid may be fufficient to fhew, that the *uniformity of profeſſion* he would contend for, cannot poffibly fubfift without an uniformity of *faith:* for as the *profeſſion,* which is to be *uniform,* muft be a *profeſſion of faith,* the difficulty will always remain, and we fhall never be able to get clear of it fo long as we have any religion or confcience left.

In fhort——Our Articles are articles of *doctrine;* and therefore every declaration of *unfeigned aſſent and confent* to them, ftrictly implies a *belief* of them: when the author, therefore, infinuates that *a man, for pru-*

dential reasons, may honestly subscribe and submit to the use of one established form, though he, in his private opinion, may think another to be better, he might have said in other words, "a man may honestly de-clare that he believes what he does not believe:" nay, that he believes such things, as no man can be an honest christian without believing, whether he declares it publicly or not.

Before I drop this subject, I must humbly take the leave of remonstrating to the author, that he knows all these shifts and evasions to be insufficient—For if a clergyman may *profess* what he does not *believe*; or if a subscription for peace-sake to an established form be all that is required, what makes him so restless? why would he alter the *things themselves*, when he confesses himself to be *pretty easy* in having assented only to *the use* of them? would he set his brethren right in articles of faith? No: that scheme is both *useless* and *impracticable:* yet, in contradiction to this principle, it is the purpose of his whole book to proselyte the church of

Ireland

Ireland to his own private sentiments, and (as hath already been observed in the *Preface*) he hopes to see them adopted as a *part of the established religion*.

But error is seldom so happy as to be consistent with itself; and from these contradictory principles, when laid together, it appears, that articles of faith, if drawn up according to his fancy, *are* necessary enough; but if published by the general assent of the church, and comprehending the doctrine of the purest ages, they are *not* necessary.

The subject of a *fraudulent subscription* having been largely and fully treated by Dr. *Waterland*, and that in a much better manner than I can ever hope to insist upon it, I refer the reader to his *Case of* Arian *Subscription*, and the *Supplement* to it, which have, and always may give general satisfaction upon this point; and if the author had read them, he might have found a much greater difficulty in making himself, as he hath done, so *easy* under these circumstances.

Having thus endeavoured to misrepresent the *subscription* of the Protestant clergy, in order to lessen the obligation of it, he proceeds to set that of the *Nicene* bishops in the same light; that their subscription, when falsely charged with the same frauds, and degraded to a like insignificancy, may keep his own in countenance. He tells us, that at the council of *Nice*, the Emperor Constantine *allowed every one to put* their own sense *upon the word* consubstantial, *and not the sense that was intended by the compilers of the creed: and accordingly*, Eusebius, *Bishop of* Cæsarea, *though he at first refused subscribing, yet when he was allowed to interpret the word* consubstantial, *as meaning* ONLY, *that the Son was not of the same substance with the creatures that were made by him;* he then *subscribed it, and so, in a little time after did* Arius [p]. I will not say, that I *suspect* all this to be false, because I can *prove*, that there is not one word of truth in it, from the beginning to end; which the author, perhaps being conscious of, has spared us the trouble of being referred to his authorities. For

[p] P. 10.

For in the first place, the Emperor did not allow any of the subscribers to put a sense upon the word *consubstantial*, different from that intended by the compilers of the creed; and it would have been very strange, if he had instructed the Bishops how to understand a creed of their own compiling, being then but a *catechumen*, and neither then nor ever after so assuming as he is here represented. The word (Homoöusios) *consubstantial*, was added to the creed by general consent, and is explained, not as meaning ONLY, *that the Son was not of the same substance with the creatures that were made by him*; but, according to the express words of *Eusebius*, which I here give at length, *that the Son of God hath no community with, or resemblance to created beings; but that* in every respect *he is like to the Father only, who hath begotten him; and that he does exist of* NO OTHER SUBSTANCE OR ESSENCE BUT OF THE FATHER. *To this* (adds *Eusebius*) thus explained *we thought good to give our assent; more especially, because we also knew, that some of the ancient learned and eminent Bishops and writers have made*

made use of this term Homoöusios, *in their explications of the divinity of the Father and of the Son. Thus much therefore we have said concerning the creed published (at* Nice*) to which* WE ALL AGREED, *not inconsiderately and without examination, but according to the* SENSES GIVEN, *which were discussed in the presence of our most pious Emperor, and for the reasons aforementioned received with unanimous consent* [q]. This is part of a letter written by *Eusebius* * himself; in which

---

[q] Socrat. Hist. Lib. 1. ch. 8.

* If the reader desires to see a farther vindication of our *Eusebius*, as Mr. *Whiston* is pleased to call him, let him consult *A second Review of Mr.* WHISTON'*s Account of primitive Doxologies* p. 19. The author of this pamphlet and of the *Review* which preceded it, was Mr. *Thirlby*, a very young man, who exposed the unfair practices and mistakes of Mr. *Whiston*, with great learning and force of argument, so as to reduce the importance of his character in the eyes of the publick. Mr. *Thirlby* was supposed to have been very much assisted in his criticisms, by the able and learned Dr. *Asheton* of *Cambridge*, who could never be prevailed upon to publish any thing as from himself. Dr. *Cave* has an express dissertation upon the supposed *Arianism* of *Eusebius*, at the latter end of the 2d vol. of his *Historia Literaria*; in which the character of that Father is very sufficiently vindicated against the misrepresentations of *Le Clerc*, a disappointed *Hugonot*, who had strong prejudices against the clergy, and in his notions bordered very nearly upon *Free thinking.*

there is no appearance either that the subscription of this learned Bishop was fraudulent, or that the Emperor indulged the subscribers with private senses of their own: for it is expresly said, that the Bishops present at the *Nicene* council subscribed the Creed according to senses *given and agreed upon* publickly; five only, out of three hundred and eighteen, being of the *Arian* opinion. The author's representation of this affair, so different from the real fact, will be a sufficient excuse for us, if we exclaim in the words of bishop *Bull, quis cordatus fidem habebit* mendacissimo *isti hominum generi*[r]?

But the account now before us will make it necessary to proceed a little farther: for the subscription of *Arius* is mentioned in so artful a manner, and shuffled in with that of *Eusebius*, as to make inexperienced readers believe they were both of the same complexion: whereas *Eusebius* assented to the consubstantiality of the Son in terms sufficiently clear and strong; but *Arius* under a very detestable subterfuge.

[r] Def. Fid. Nic. p. 144. § 4.

fuge. We are told, that he wrote down his own heretical doctrine upon a piece of paper, which he concealed in his bosom; then appeared boldly before the Emperor, subscribed the Creed, and took a solemn oath, that he did really believe—*as he had written*[¹]. This done, the Emperor dismissed him with these words. "If thy faith is right, thou hast done well in swearing to it; but if it be still wicked, and thou hast sworn notwithstanding, may God take vengeance on thee for thy oath [*]." It will not be amiss here to add the concluding part of *Arius*'s history; which I shall relate in the words of the very learned and pious Dr. *Cave*, referring my reader, for the truth of the relation, to the authorities quoted in his margin, most of which I have taken the pains to consult for myself. The business of *Arius* his subscription was transacted on a *Saturday*; and in virtue of it, *Alexander* the bishop

---

[¹] Socrat. Lib. I. cap. penult.

[*] Ει ορθη σε ιsιν η πιsις, καλως ωμοσας· ει δε ασεβης εsιν η πιsις Cε, και ωμοσας, ο Θεος ιν τε ορκε κρινει τα καλα Cε. *Athanaſ.* Epiſt. ad Serap.

of *Conſtantinople* was enjoined to receive him the next day to communion. But
" that very evening, or, as others report,
" the next morning, *Arius* going through
" the ſtreets with a pompous train of his
" friends and followers, ſwelled with the
" hopes of to-morrow's triumphs, was
" come to a place in *Conſtantine's Forum*,
" when he found himſelf neceſſitated to
" enquire for a place of eaſement, where
" his ſpirits ſuddenly failing, the fate of
" treacherous and apoſtate *Judas* became
" his portion, he fell headlong, and burſt-
" ing aſunder in the midſt, immediately
" expired. *Socrates* and others ſay, that
" the bowels, and all the *inteſtina*, with a
" vaſt flux of blood iſſued out. His friends
" impatiently expect his return, till it
" ſeeming longer than ordinary, ſome went
" to call him, and *Euſebius* †, more for-
" ward than the reſt, reproached his back-
" wardneſs and neglect both of his friends
" and himſelf; but hearing no anſwer,
" they went in, and there found the wretch
" wallowing in his own filth and blood.
" His

† Of *Nicomedea*.

"His followers were strangely surprized "with the accident, which they could "not but look upon as a fatal blow to their "cause; though, to cover as much as "might be the shame and terror of so in- "famous a death, they fled to their old "refuge of lies and falsehood, giving it "out, that his death was procured by sor- "cery and magic arts.—Thus died *Arius*, "the great incendiary of the church; and "happy had it been, had his schism and "his principles died with him ‡."

I had flattered myself that the advocates of *Arius* his doctrine would have left his *person* to that infamy, from which they have never attempted to retrieve it, without giving the cause, in some respect, or other, a worse look than it had before. But in the first volume of *Mosheim's* Ecclesiastical History, translated by Mr. *Maclaine*, minister of the English Church at the *Hague*, there occurred to me the following reflexion on the death of this Archheretic in a note of the translator. "After "having considered this matter with the "utmost

‡ Cave's Lives of the Fathers. Fol. edit. 4. p. 382.

"utmost care, it appears to me extremely
"probable, that this unhappy man was a
"victim to the resentment of his enemies,
"and was destroyed by poison, or some
"such violent method. A blind and fa-
"natical zeal for certain systems of faith,
"has in all ages produced such horrible
"acts of cruelty and injustice *." By what
steps the author discovered this *extreme probability*, it doth not appear. The Ecclesiastical Histories and writings of the fathers, have been open to other readers; and antiquity never furnished them with any evidence whereupon such a conjecture might be grounded. Indeed this writer doth not pretend to any; and it is plain he never found any, by his laying this black indictment in such vague and general terms, "poison *or some such* violent method." But the circumstances of his death are not to be reconciled either with poison or any other method of human violence. He was to all appearance in health and high spirits a few minutes before the accident: and besides, we know of no poison that can expel

* P. 219. n. y.

pel the entrails. If he had been affaffinated, his own followers, by the principal of whom he was attended in the inftant after his death, muft have difcovered marks of violence upon his body; and they wanted neither fagacity nor malice to make the moft of any fuch appearance. Nothing remains then, but the aftrology and artmagic of the perfecuted *Athanafius*; by imputing it to which, whatever may be pretended by the *Arians* of this age, the *Arians* of that have given us their own teftimony that his death was *fupernatural*. The circumftances of his death were notorious throughout the whole city of *Conftantinople*, and, as *Socrates* adds, in a manner throughout the whole world: the Emperor was very much alarmed, and his own party for a while were confounded, all men looking upon it as an inftance of remarkable vengeance immediately fallen upon him from heaven. This, however, is a perfuafion of the ancients, which, as Mr. *Maclaine* thinks, will find " but lit-
" tle credit in thefe times." That may be: but then if the incredulity of this age is

to be admitted as a teſt of falſehood, we muſt do juſtice on the other ſide, and admit the credulity of the age (credulous enough on ſome ſubjects) as a teſt of truth: then we may ſhut up our books, and leave incredulity to determine, that *Arius* did not die by the judgment of God; while credulity affirms, without reaſon or evidence, that he was actually murdered by the bloody-minded orthodox. This method, for the brevity of it, will be extremely convenient, and will give an entire new face to the whole hiſtory of the ancient church.

The ſuppoſed murder of *Arius* then hath nothing to reſt upon but the following reflexion, which is improperly worded and very injuriouſly applied: " a blind and fa-
" natical zeal for certain ſyſtems of faith
" has in all ages produced ſuch horrible
" acts of cruelty and injuſtice." Syſtems of *error*, ſuch as the heathen ſyſtem, the Apoſtate-Jewiſh ſyſtem, the *Arian*, and the *Papal* ſyſtems; theſe, and not that ſyſtem of *faith* which the fathers of the *Nicene* council had derived from Chriſt and his

his Apoſtles, have been followed with a *blind* and *fanatical zeal:* and as men *perſecute others* only when they cannot *juſtify themſelves,* all theſe ſyſtems being defective in point of reaſon and argument, could never put up with contradiction, and were therefore productive of the moſt horrible acts of cruelty and injuſtice, to which may be added all the exceſſes of lying and calumniating: while the orthodox faith, from the firſt planting of chriſtianity, inſtead of perſecuting, hath been expoſed in all ages as the object of malice and perſecution to other ſyſtems. If the *Nicene* chriſtians had torn the fleſh of Pagans from their bones and roaſted them alive upon gridirons, had crucified the Jews, and drawn together five thouſand armed ſoldiers to force *Athanaſius* upon the church, as the *Arians* did to drive him out and aſſaſſinate him, &c. &c. they might then have been naturally enough ſuſpected of other acts of cruelty and injuſtice; though ſuch a ſuſpicion would not be a ſufficient warrant with hiſtorians of credit for charging them with any particular act without

ſome

some particular evidence, of which, in this case, the author hath not produced one syllable; but hath only shewed us the strength of his wishes and the bias of his inclinations. The seditious practices of *Arius*, his life, the impiety and ill effects of his doctrine, together with the terror and infamy of his death, have reflected so little credit upon his party, that they are tempted to blanch his history at the expence of the orthodox. This however is not to be done by a stratagem so barefaced as that of the learned Mr. *Mosheim*'s translator: for although the credulity of some men, in such matters as make *against* the church, is now risen to an extravagant height; there are many still left, who are not quite supple enough to take an author's *bare word* for a *capital* crime, supposed to have been committed *fourteen hundred years before he was born*; and this against all the reason and circumstances of the fact, together with the express testimony of the age in which it happened. If this be the way of improving an history of the church, I shall expect shortly to see some annotator rife up and do juſtice to the character of *Judas:* whoſe death having been attended with the *Arian* ſymptom of his *bowels guſhing out,* on which account *Epiphanius* ſcruples not to obſerve that *Arius* died, καθαπερ κ̓ Ιȣδας πο]ε, *as* Judas *did of old;* it may appear *extremely probable* to a perſon who conſiders the matter with *the utmoſt care,* that he died by *poiſon or ſome ſuch violent method,* and was a *victim* to the *blind* reſentment of St. *Peter* and the other apoſtles in their *fanatical zeal!* I repreſent theſe things, not out of any hatred or contempt for the perſons of the *Arians,* but that they may ſtop a little and conſider, to what groundleſs, indeed to what iniquitous, ſhifts they are driven to varniſh a bad cauſe, not to be maintained but by calumny, clamour, or violence; and theſe are not the marks either of truth or of chriſtianity.

We are now returning again to the *act of uniformity;* the author of the Eſſay having imagined that "theſe words *to the uſe* " *of* were omitted with deſign" (in the declaration) " as a ſnare to oblige *poor con-* " *ſcientious*

"*scientious men* to give up their livings:" and accordingly he tells us, "there were 1800 persons deprived of their livings, rather than submit to the terms prescribed."ᶦ Now supposing all this to be true, the cause for which *he* is pleading can receive no advantage by it; as it never was espoused, to the best of my knowledge, by any one of the persons thus deprived: and I make no doubt but that many of them would rather have submitted to be burnt alive than subscribe to the doctrines advanced in an *Essay on Spirit*. But to speak the truth, the characters of these poor conscientious men, and the circumstances of their deprivation are scandalously misreported to bring an odium on the *act of uniformity* and the present *constitution* of the church of *England*. This is the scope of all that superabundance of *charity* affected by this writer; who ought to be reminded, that when charity is all of it placed in one of the scales, and there is not a drachm left in the other, it is no longer charity but *partiality* and *injustice*.

ᶦ P. 13.

The moſt authentic account of the expulſion of the *Calviniſtical* miniſters by the *act of uniformity* after the *Reſtoration*, is delivered down to us by the earl of *Clarendon*; whoſe credit as an hiſtorian is too well eſtabliſhed to need any of my recommendations; and that he was furniſhed with the beſt materials cannot be queſtioned; himſelf having been the principal agent in the tranſactions of that time.

The caſe is related by our author with theſe three circumſtances. 1ſt. that the number of the deprived miniſters was 1800. 2dly, that they were *poor conſcientious men:* and 3dly, that the declaration which required their *aſſent to all things* in the *Common Prayer* was the reaſon of their nonconformity.

1. As to their *number,* the noble hiſtorian aſſures us, that the preſbyterians themſelves, in their petition to the king againſt the act of uniformity, made it "*five times more than was true;*"[a] and that "the greateſt of theſe miniſters, after ſome "time" (when the contributions of their own faction began to ſlacken) "ſubſcribed to

---

[a] Contin. of *Clarendon's* Life. p. 157.

"to those very declarations, which they had urged as the greatest motives to their non-conformity. And the number was *very small* and of *very weak and inconsiderable men*, that continued refractory and received no charge in the church."*

2. The following extract will shew how far they deserved the character of *poor* and *conscientious*. "There was scarce a man in that number, who had not been so great a promoter of the rebellion, or contributed so much to it, that they had no other title to their lives but the king's mercy; and there were very few amongst them, who had not come into the possession of the churches they now held, by the expulsion of the orthodox ministers who were lawfully possessed of them, and who being by their imprisonment, poverty, and other kinds of oppression and contempt during so many years, departed this life, the usurpers remained undisturbed in their livings, and thought it now the highest tyranny to be removed from them, though for offending the law, and disobedience to the government."ˣ

Then

*Ibid. P. 161. ˣ P. 157.

Then thirdly, though it be true that they were offended by the declaration mentioned by the author, it is false that this was the whole ground of their non-conformity, or, as he expresses it, the *snare* that *obliged* these *poor conscientious men* to *give up their livings:* for the act of uniformity contained another declaration, which required them to renounce their *solemn league* and *covenant*; and their zeal to this bloody engagement was at least as strong as their aversion to the liturgy. This appears from the words of their own inflammatory exhortations to their proselytes, whose old animosities, then very likely to subside, they endeavoured to keep alive by assuring them, that " they could not with " a good conscience subscribe either the " one or the other declaration : they could " not say, that they did assent or consent " in the first, nor declare in the second, " that there remained *no obligation from* " *the covenant.*"ʸ For a farther account of these men and the times in which they lived, I refer the reader to the earl of Clarendon's

ʸ 156.

rendon's history of his own life; a work which of late years hath done so much honour to the *Oxford* press. He will there see the workings of different factions, and the effects of different principles, on the peace, order, and prosperity of the commonwealth. I mention this work of *Clarendon* in a more particular manner, because I saw it lately declared in a newspaper by some outrageous libertine, who being employed in propagating the old rebellious principles of that age, would have all their horrible consequences buried in oblivion, that his writings ought to be *burnt by the hands of the common hangman.* In return to which, I shall only say for myself, that if any production of mine should ever be worthy of so great an honour, I could wish it might live and die (by any kind of death) with the writings of the earl of *Clarendon.*

I have already taken some notice of a sarcasm upon the orthodoxy of this church, which in the judgment of the *Essayist* is no more than *imaginary orthodoxy*. How far the reformers of our liturgy were carried by by their *imaginations*, he does not exprefly fay: but from the temper of his phrafeology and the latitude of his expreffion, it is eafy enough to forfee that there will be fomething new and curious, when he comes to explain his fentiments concerning *orthodoxy*, together with its oppofites, *herefy* and *fchifm*.

Firſt then, for his *orthodoxy*; which *according to the* common fenfe *of the word, is conftituted by the eftablifhed religion of any country: and hence it comes to pafs, that a perfon may be efteemed as very* orthodox *in* England *or* Ireland, *who would be deemed as an* heretic *at* Rome, *or in other countries*"́. Orthodoxy then, is nothing fix'd and ſtated, but changes its nature according to the different temper of the climate it refides in, and *Chameleon*-like, can affume any colour it chances to fit upon, and ſtill be as good *orthodoxy* as it was before. This, it feems, is gathered from the *common fenfe* of the word: but if what is here taken as the common fenfe of orthodoxy, be an *erroneous* or *abufed fenfe*, nothing but error can be

" Ded. p. 23, 24.

be inferred from it. And that it is such, must be evident to every one who is able to construe the *Greek* (ορθοδοξια) or knows that in the primitive ages, it was used only to denote *the right opinion*, that is, the Christian faith in general, as received in the Catholic church planted by the apostles, which, in their days, was one and the same all the world over: and none but the faithful members of this *one* communion were termed *orthodox*. To this purpose Theodoret observes, τῳ υπερ των αποστολικων δογμαῖων αγωνιζομενῳ, ορθοδοξῶ ονομα˟, *we call him orthodox, who earnestly contends for the apostolic doctrines*, that is, *the faith once delivered to the saints* by the Apostles. Thus also, when it is said of the three thousand converted *Jews*[z], that *they continued steadfastly in the Apostles doctrine and fellowship*, it is perfectly the same, as if they had been declared, in one word, to have been *orthodox:* and therefore, every particular church now subsisting in the world, is *more* or *less* orthodox, in proportion as it approaches nearer to, or is more remote from, the purity of the apostolic times.

But,

[x] Pref. ad Dial.   [z] Acts ii. 42.

But, on the contrary, if any point of doctrine, whether right or wrong, may, by a strange abuse of the word, be esteemed *orthodox*, because it makes a part of the *established religion of any country*; then the author's definition, if admitted and applied, will prove that any particular church may be *orthodox*, where it is *heterodox*; which is, what we commonly call, a contradiction in terms. And yet, proceeding upon a fallacy so easily detected, he descants, thro' twenty pages, upon the crime of *heresy*; measuring it all the way, by this false rule of equivocal orthodoxy, and setting it forth as an insignificant deviation from any established form, which, as it happens, may be sometimes right, and sometimes wrong. I will run over these pages, and extract in short, as well as I can, the sum of that doctrine they contain.

Accordingly, I find, that six of them* may be reduced to the following propositions—The Christianity of the Apostles, was, by the blind Scribes and Pharisees of the *Jews*, called *heresy*—and therefore, *it is*

---

* From p. 22. to 28.

is *possible that an heretic may be in the right.*

No; nothing can possibly be inferred from hence, but that a person who is *in the right*, may be *falsely called* an heretic by those who are *in the wrong*.

In the course of these observations upon heresy, he is pleased to produce a text from St. *Paul,* in which, by the assistance of a large comment, the Apostle is tortured till he delivers a very singular account of this crime, together with the reasons for which the church is empowered to inflict a punishment upon those that are guilty of it: an account, so foreign from the purpose of that glorious instrument of the Holy Spirit, that I dare be confident, he would rather have suffered martyrdom, than have submitted to deliver it. The text is this—*A man that is an* heretic, *after the first and second admonition, reject: knowing that he that is such, is subverted, and sinneth, being condemned of himself*[b]. From which the author presumes in his comment, that an heretic is such, not for the sake of any destructive

[b] Tit. iii. 10, 11.

ſtructive opinion he maintains in oppoſition to the truth, and to the extreme peril of his own ſoul, but that *he ſinneth, by perſevering therein after admonition*; and that this *perverſeneſs of his will, not the error of his judgment, is the cauſe and foundation of his excommunication* [c].

So that it is the *admonition* an heretic receives from the church, which makes him become guilty of that very crime, for which he is *admoniſhed!* and he commences a compleat heretic immediately upon his excommunication, and not before: becauſe, if it is the eccleſiaſtical cenſure which renders him guilty, his guilt muſt increaſe with the ſeverity of that cenſure; and when the cenſure hath ariſen to its full growth, the crime likewiſe muſt have done the ſame. But a ſmall attention to this matter will enable us to perceive, that here we have a falſe account of *ſchiſm*, inſtead of a true account of *hereſy*; and that upon this the author proceeds in what follows.

For it is declared moreover in theſe words of St. *Paul*, that an heretic is *ſelf-condemn'd*;

at

[c] P. 28, 29.

at which paſſage we are directed by a very judicious marginal reference, to *Acts* xiii. 46. where *Paul* and *Barnabas* tell the *Jews*, upon their rejecting the Chriſtian faith, that they *judged themſelves unworthy of everlaſting life*. This therefore was ſuppoſed by thoſe pious men, who made the reference, to contain that very ſentence of condemnation, which an heretic paſſes upon himſelf: But the eſſay writer, agreeable to his uſual method of taking the perſpective by the wrong end, diminiſhes it down to a petty conviction only, of his wilful *perſeverance in oppoſition to the church*; which expoſition does not touch upon the meaning of the text; ſince, in other words, it will ſtand thus—*An heretic is ſenſible that he is condemned by the church*—whereas, on the contrary, the Apoſtle has aſſerted in terms, that he is *condemned by himſelf*; that is, he is ſenſible of his guilt, and accuſed by his own conſcience. From the whole of what our author hath ſaid upon this ſubject, we may collect this unſcriptural definition of hereſy—It is an offence, not againſt the revealed will of God, and the

concerns

concerns of eternity; but against the will of man, and the outward forms of society; not against the faith, but against the church that abides by it. Which, in effect, is to suggest, that the church sanctifies the faith; whereas, on the other hand, it is always taken for granted, that the faith sanctifies the church.

And what are the motives which excite him thus to diminish this vice and improve it, if possible, by *speaking smooth things and prophesying deceits* about it, almost into a christian virtue? Why it seems the words *schismatic* and *heretic, are sounds, which, ever since the days of* Popery, *occasion wondrous horror in the ears of the vulgar*[d]. And as he is apprehensive, that many of his brethren, upon discovering his attempt to corrupt the doctrines of the church, and disturb the peace of it, will load him with these opprobrious names, he esteems it his interest to explain away their true meaning, and to brand those with the name of superstitious and papistical *vulgar*, who shall apply to him in their proper sense, such nauseous

[d] P. 19.

feous appellations. By this means, whatever noife they may chance to make in *his ears*, he may contemplate his own interpretation of them, and continue to enjoy his repofe.

I cannot better obviate thefe dangerous infinuations, than by fetting down a true defcription of *herefy*, as it ftands in the Holy Scriptures; which being dictated by the infallible Spirit of God, and written before the *days of popery*, cannot be charged with inflaming the account of any vice, or of adulterating its own divine truth with any hot and impure fpirits, diftilled therefrom in after-ages, by the fuperftitious church of *Rome*. To proceed then—

2 Pet. ii. 1. *There fhall be falfe teachers among you, who privily fhall bring in damnable herefies,* or (αιρεσεις απωλειας) *herefies of deftruction*. Herefies, therefore, are *damnable*; that is, they lead their advocates and propagators to *deftruction*; and in general they are *privily brought in,* (παρεισαξυσιν) they are carried round about, and introduced at fome private entrance; they do not make their approach with that undifguifed ho-

E   nefty,

nesty, which fears no discovery; but steal into the houshold of faith——under the masque of conscience.

The apostle goes on—*even denying the Lord that bought them*—yea, these *false teachers* shall, to compleat their guilt, *even* dare to deny the Lord that *bought them*; either by rejecting the ransom he hath condescended to pay for them, or by disowning that he, who paid that ransom, was *the* LORD.

The remaining part of the verse declares, that they *shall bring upon themselves swift destruction*. Though for a short time they may escape the terror of an earthly tribunal, yet the eye of God can penetrate into the inmost recesses of their hearts; and his arm will at length drag them forth from their hiding places, to appear at the bar of his tribunal, whose mercy and long-suffering they have abused and affronted: though they may delude themselves with a vain presumption that they can contradict God, and yet be in the right; that the matter they are upon is *barely speculative*, and such as God careth not for; yet if their crime be such as the apostle here means to describe, their *judgment now of a long time lingereth not, and their damnation slumbereth not.*

In 1 *Tim.* iv. 1. Heretics, or those who depart from the truth, and follicit others to *follow their pernicious ways,* are called *seducing spirits,* or persons actuated by that original seducer, who first tempted man to apostatize from the wisdom of God, and to follow his own lascivious fancy, in contradiction to an express command of his maker: their heresies are termed *doctrines of devils,* invented by the adversary, and set up as rivals to the pure and saving doctrines of *Christ*; and those who set forth and propagate such doctrines, are declared to be *ministers of Satan*[*], artfully substituting and diligently preaching his word of death, instead of the *word of life*; nay proceeding so far as to call the former by the name of the latter, that they may render it the more palatable, and tempt their hearers to swallow down such poisonous impurities with greediness.

This

[*] 2 Cor. xi. 15.

This I take to be the true account of heresy, because the scripture gives it me, and because I find it insisted upon as such by all the pious writers of the ancient church, now so much despised and neglected: and if it is the true, surely we ought to tremble at seeing this destructive evil artfully recommended to the world, under the soft phrases of *an opinion barely speculative, a different mode of thinking!* If *an heretic* means no more than *one of a different opinion from the majority*[f], whether that majority think right or wrong; if, I say, this reasoning be true, then the scriptures are false; and it is of no importance whether a man be a christian or a mahometan.

As I have alluded to the term, *barely speculative*, it may not be amiss more fully to remark this *writer's* strange misapplication of it: for by *opinions barely speculative*, he would have us understand the chief and fundamental mysteries of the christian faith; nay, that very root and stock, from whence groweth all moral obligation to us

as

[f] P. 32.

as *Chriſtians*, all ſtrength and comfort in this world, and all our hope of everlaſting ſalvation in the next? All this, as depending upon the *doctrine of the Trinity*, is, it ſeems, nothing but a mere lifeleſs theory, an empty ſubject for the mind to exerciſe its curioſity upon, and concerning which, it may think and imagine for itſelf with as great freedom, as it does about any baſeleſs and airy fabric of modern *metaphyſics*. But it is evident that the ſcriptures give no warrant to this diſtinction of *ſpeculative* and *practical* duties; for when the *Jews* put the following queſtion to *Chriſt—What ſhall we do that we might* work *the* works *of God?* his anſwer was—*This is the* work *of God, that ye* believe *on him whom he hath ſent.* Where then is the difference between faith and works?

Since the principles of the chriſtian faith, in common with thoſe of all other religions, are (in the author's opinion) *barely ſpeculative*; he ſeems to wonder that *men ſhould be more diſpleaſed with one another for any difference of opinion about them, than for their being of different ſizes or complexions*; and obſerves, that *for this, no reaſon in general*

ral can indeed be affigned[e]. The *fact* however is not to be disputed: and that we may not be at a loss for the *reasons*, let us first consider the case of the *heterodox*. Truth and falsehood differ in themselves as really as light and darkness. In common life this difference discovers itself in their effects. The Gospel assures us, that a *corrupt tree cannot bring forth good fruit*; therefore it is impossible that error in religion can be productive of peace, order, charity, and subjection for conscience sake; or that it can cease to be productive of hatred, malice, rage, and cruelty, so far as it hath an opportunity of following its inclinations. Bigotry to Paganism made the heathens persecute the christians, because the fabulous characters and attributes of *Jupiter*, *Mars*, *Bacchus*, and *Venus* could not be vindicated by other methods. Among christians persecution never found encouragement till they had errors to support by it. Papists do not burn a protestant because he disbelieves the Trinity or the Incarnation, but because he denies the *corporal presence*,

[e] Ded. p. 33.

presence, the *worship of Images*, the vicarial character of the *Bishop of Rome*, &c. &c. In a word, truth defends itself by *reason* and *patient suffering*; error by *violence* and *cruelty*: and so there is a very particular reason why men who are grosly mistaken are *displeased* with others who *differ from them in opinion*.

There is also some displeasure on the part of the *orthodox*, for which they are not to be blamed, unless it degenerates into malice and hatred. Our blessed Saviour was pleased to express his approbation of the church of *Ephesus* in these words— *Thou canst not bear them which are evil; and thou hast tried them which say they are apostles, and are not; and hast found them lyars*[h]. St. *John* hath instructed us, that *whosoever abideth not in the* doctrine *of* Christ, *is not to be received by us into our houses, neither are we to bid him God speed*, (that is, we are not in any wise to encourage his attempt, or promote the success of it) *for he that biddeth him God speed, is partaker of his evil deeds*[i]. And our blessed Lord admonished

[h] Rev. ii. 2. [i] 2 John ix. 10, 11.

nished his apostles, that if any one *neglect to hear the church, he should be unto them as an heathen man and a publican*; adding withal (on a very proper occasion) that divine authority upon which the church is to proceed—*Whatsoever ye shall bind on earth, shall be bound in heaven, and whatsoever ye shall loose on earth, shall be loosed in heaven*[k]. It is now thought expedient that we should entertain very moderate and qualified sentiments about such passages as these; yet, we must not forget, that in the scriptures, there are such.

Seeing, therefore, it is absolutely requisite that there should be a proper distinction preserved between such as are humble and believing, and such as are refractory and unbelieving, lest by encouraging the guilty, the innocent should partake of their crimes, and help to spread the infection; it is somewhat strange that the *Reverend Essay-writer* should spend several pages in the unnatural endeavour of bringing about a coalition between *Christians, Jews, Turks, Infidels,* and *Heretics*; not considering,

[k] Matt. xviii. 17, 18.

ing, that amongst such, it is impossible there should be any community of sentiment, or any hearty reconciliation. For if those who are on the right side are quiet and at rest, those on the wrong, are, through the implacable spirit of him that *from the beginning was a murderer,* so restless and impatient of contradiction, that they never will, or can be; and for the truth of this, I might appeal to the testimony of all ages.

There is a very plain rule, of resting upon the *most certain warrants of holy scripture,* and of having such a degree of charity for mankind, as to encourage none of them in sin; but this the author will not attend to; chusing rather to descant upon *fire* and *faggot,* as the sanction of human appointments in the church of *Rome;* as if there could be no difference between just reprehension for sin, and unjust persecution for righteousness sake: and on the other side, he takes great pains to recommend such a species of charity, as would obliterate the distinction between good and evil. His own charity however, hath not
with-

with-held him from fome very abfurd and unjuft reflexions, of which the following is a fpecimen: for as the *conduct of mankind* (it fhould be *of Chriftians) is quite otherways* in this refpect; that is, as they fometimes difagree, and will have *no fellowfhip with the unfruitful works of darknefs, but rather reprove them*; he thinks this can be *attributed to nothing but* a vicious pride *in our natures, which gives us an averfion for every one that differs in opinion from us*.

If every man was left to make his own religion, and religion were nothing but *opinion,* then every man would have a right to be indulged in his own way: but if God hath publifhed a religion from heaven, and commanded all men to leave their own inventions and fubmit to what is revealed, the cafe alters very much. Then any man who troubles a chriftian fociety with the irreligious productions of his own brain, is both a blameable and a dangerous perfon. It may be obferved in the phrafe of this writer, that the Devil *differs in opinion* from many Chriftians, he hates

hates the doctrines of the *incarnation*, the *satisfaction*, the *adoration of Jesus Christ*, and *submission to the will of God*. For these differences of opinion we may dislike the devil without any breach of charity. And should any man appear to think just as the devil does, and to speak of Jesus Christ and his redemption with more contempt than the devil ever dared to do in his own person; we should certainly be excusable if we expressed an aversion for his opinions: though every good man would at the same time commiserate his condition, and pray for his repentance and restitution.

If it were impossible to *rebuke* men *sharply* for their wickedness and infidelity without being guilty of a *vicious pride*, we should find ourselves obliged to charge some degree of this vicious pride upon the *Son of God* himself; who while his heart overflowed with tenderness for an unbelieving and abandoned nation, could yet say to them, *Ye serpents, ye generation of vipers, how can ye escape the damnation of hell?* And again, *Ye are of your father the devil.* St. *Paul* in like manner said to the *Jews*
who

who refused to hear him, *Your blood be upon your own heads;* and, on another occasion, he hath this severe reflection concerning some, who by false doctrines made Christ of none effect: *I would they were even cut off, which trouble you.*

St. *Ignatius,* cautioning the Christians of *Smyrna* against some who preached a doctrine now maintained by the *Quakers,* speaks in this plain manner; " I arm you " beforehand against certain *beasts in the* " *shape of men*[1], whom you must not only " not receive, but if it be possible must not " meet with: only you must *pray for them,* " that if it be the will of God, they may " repent, which yet will be very hard." No Christian will presume to say, that *Christ,* or St. *Paul,* or the primitive *Martyrs,* were either mistaken in the notion, or deficient in the practice of true charity: therefore charity doth not consist in a sceptical indifference toward all opinions, but may stand well enough with some of that zeal which ill men are always ready enough to exert in opposition to the *faith once delivered*

---

[1] Θηρίων των ἀνθρωπομορφων

livered to the saints. It may seem to argue a spirit of benevolence and liberality in the eyes of the ignorant, if we pass over all the false opinions of the world: but it is every man's duty to take care, lest while he is affecting humility toward his fellow-creatures, he should be so saucy to his maker as to assume a dispensing power over the divine laws; and by flattering other men in their sins, should be made a partaker in the guilt and punishment of them, while he hath already too many of his own to answer for.

In this dedicatory introduction to his Essay, our author hath several *pleas (arguments* I will not call them) by which he would countenance his plan for reforming the doctrine of the Trinity, as it stands at present in our creeds and articles. It remains, therefore, that I extract these, and give them their answers separately according to that order in which they occur.

Plea I. " If the church be not infallible
" any more than the state, why may not
" that be amended as well as the state? And
" why should we be more afraid of break-
" ing

" ing the peace of the church than of the
" ftate? the peace of the one being full
" as neceffary to be preferved, as the peace
" of the other ⁿ."

No juft parallel can, I think, be drawn between the fallibility, or infallibility of the church, and of the ftate, fince they are not directed by the fame rule, and are converfant about matters greatly differing from each other: the one about invariable truths, which concern the everlafting happinefs of man, and are determined by divine revelation; the other about national or political principles of its own devifing, which, fo far as they are built upon human authority or national compact, may be varied at pleafure, as the different exigencies of times and occafions fhall require; fo far as they partake, in common with the ecclefiaftical rule, of divine authority, thefe are as unalterable as the other. If, therefore, it can be clearly proved that any *human errors* have crept into the church, any pofitions *contradicting* the word of truth, let them, in God's name, be reformed: but as to the
essential

ⁿ P. 21, 22.

essential articles, or substance of the christian faith, it must for ever remain as the scriptures have fixed it.

Plea II. "I am under less apprehension "for the church than for the state; for as "to the christian religion in general, we "have the sure word of prophecy, that "the gates of hell shall not prevail against "it; and as to particular establishments, I "should apprehend, that the freer they "were from errors, the more likely they "would be to stand*." Tis true, a candlestick with a light burning in it may be removed from one part of the house to another, without extinguishing the light; but, yet, the apartment from which it is removed, having no light but what it received from it, will be left in the dark. The light of christianity will always burn *somewhere* till the end of the world; but no particular church or nation can from this prophecy receive any well grounded encouragement to tamper with the faith, through a vain presumption of its continuance, although the members of that church, under the
specious

* P. 45.

specious pretence of snuffing the candle, are continually endeavouring to put it out. Suppose the christian religion, when expelled from *Great-Britain*, should settle whole and entire in the city of *Amsterdam*, it would give us but cold comfort to reflect, that though the christian religion *in particular* had left us, yet the christian religion *in general* was still subsisting somewhere in the world.

Before any *particular establishment is freed from its errors*, we must ask, who is to judge of those errors? A council of learned and pious men, assembling in the fear of God, or one solitary objector, who is pleased to think that such reformers complied so far with *the humour of the times*[p] in which they lived, as not to have effected a *thorough reformation?* If we admit the *author's* judgment, we shall have that very doctrine (with many more) expunged as an error, by a departure from which a way was prepared in the eastern churches, for that desolation brought upon them by the imposture of *Mahomet*; which prevailed only in

those

[p] P. 19.

thofe parts of the chriftian world where *Arianifm* had firft been admitted.

Plea III. " It is manifeft that before the
" reformation took place, the fame argu-
" ments were then made ufe of, againft any
" innovations in religion that are now;
" and all alterations were as much de-
" claimed againft ᑫ."

Hence this *writer* means to infinuate, that as a reformation in religion was once made, againft an *unreafonable oppofition*, and the church freed from its errors; a reformation (how wildly foever it be demanded, or reafonably propofed) ought to be made again: that is, there always may be a reformation of a reformation; and becaufe the church, at the time here mentioned, had many errors, and was cleared of them; therefore fhe muft have many more, and may be cleared of them again. At which rate of arguing, a man may eafily prove that *Mary Magdalen* had fourteen devils; and that becaufe feven were caft out, feven more muft have ftaid behind.

Plea IV. " If a ftorm fhould arife (the
" church may run a rifque of having that
" tree

ᑫ P. 47.

"tree torn up by the roots, which might have been saved by a little pruning'."

Whence is this storm to arise? not from any *Popish* power; becaufe then the moſt adviſeable method would be, not to lop and to *prune*, but to engraft freſh branches upon the old ſtock. It is therefore to ariſe from the oppoſite quarter; that is, either from the diſſenters, or ſuch members of the church as are corrupted with the *Arian* opinions. The author, when he penned this ſuggeſtion, forgot himſelf a little; otherwiſe he would not have put ſo much *ſtorm* and *tempeſt* into the compoſition of his friends.

But what can he mean by *a little pruning?* If the *tree* here ſpoken of is the *Chriſtian Faith* at preſent growing in the church of *England,* the doctrine of a *Trinity in Unity* is the *root* of it: and whoever peruſes our *Liturgy,* will find this doctrine ſo cloſely interwoven with all the forms and offices of it, that the *Reformation* for which he is pleading can never take effect, till the tree is cut up by the root. If this ſhould

' P. 53.

should be our method of *pruning*, we shall have little to fear afterwards: for when his *tempestuous* friends come to rip and rend, there will be nothing left for them to do.

Plea V. " The most proper method that
" could be taken to render the church of
" *Ireland* truly *catholic*, would be——to
" open the gates of its communion as wide
" as was consistent with the gospel of
" Christ[*]."

How wide the *author* thinks that to be cannot exactly be determined, till he speaks more explicitly: but we ought to be very cautious how we enter upon this *widening* scheme, for fear of making a fatal mistake —for *strait is the gate which leadeth unto life*; as on the contrary, *wide is the gate which leadeth to destruction, and many there be, which go in thereat*[†]. It may be said, without giving offence to any sincere believer of the churches of *England* and *Ireland*, that if they were opened as *wide* as some of our modern reformers would have them, they might pretty much resemble those described by the poet,

——*The*

[*] Ded. p. 62.   [†] Matth. vii. 13, 14.

———*The gates wide open stood,*
That with extended wings a banner'd host
Under spread ensigns marching, might pass through
With horse and chariots rank'd in loose array[u].

As to the *Catholicism* here proposed, it is merely ideal, and all the wit of man could never reduce it to practice. For no church can subsist as such without a common form of public service; and this service must be built upon the *doctrines* received. But I desire to know, how it would be possible to frame such a service as should agree to the contrary doctrines of the *Arians, Socinians,* and *orthodox* Christians? what is *religion* to some, is *Idolatry* to others. I say nothing of the *Presbyterians, Anabaptists, Independents,* and other forms which were found so irreconcileable with each other in the age of *Catholicism,* when the gates of our communion were torn off their hinges by the Puritan faction. The experience of that age, as the distractions of it are described by *Edwards,* an honest Puritan,

[u] Par. lost, B. II. l. 884.

tan, in his *Gangræna,* ought to convince our *catholic* experimentalists, that their principles, instead of uniting men, do sow the seeds of discord so effectually, that all religion would either demolish itself, or be soon laughed out of the world, if it were to exist in the motley forms of the last century; when all the same pleas which the Presbyterians had used against the church were turned against themselves, and they had the mortification to hear the *Independents* publickly praying, that the *Presbytery might be removed, that* Christ's *kingdom* (meaning their own way) *might be set up*[w]. The dissenters therefore, if they know their own interest, will think themselves more happy and secure under a toleration, than any part of them could be under an establishment. They may *all* be tolerated, but they cannot all have the establishment: and an *equal* claim to it could only set them together by the ears, as it did before; for which themselves could find no remedy but the *Restoration.*

[w] Edwards's Gangr. Part I. p. 35.

Plea VI. 'The preface to our *Book of Common Prayer* declares, that "*the par-* "*ticular forms of divine worship, and the* "*rites and ceremonies appointed to be used* "*therein, being things in their own nature* "*indifferent and alterable, and so acknow-* "*ledged, it is but reasonable, that upon* "*weighty and important considerations, ac-* "*cording to the various exigencies of times* "*and occasions, such changes and alterations* "*may be made therein, as to those that are* "*in place and authority should, from time to* "*time, seem either necessary or expedient.*"

This passage is taken by the essay-writer in as large and unlimited a sense, as if those pious men, who reviewed our excellent Liturgy, had thereby insinuated a permission to change the essential articles of faith therein contained, according to the various humours of every age; or to alter the *doctrine of the Trinity,* &c. in such a manner, as that the Liturgy might always wear a garb suitable to the cut of the times. Their concession, will not countenance *his* proposed method of reformation, unless it be made to appear, that by such *forms of divine*

divine worſhip, rites, and ceremonies, as are in their own nature *indifferent and alterable,* they meant *Creeds, Articles,* and all other *eſſentials* of the *Liturgy;* for theſe are the points wherein he would contend for an alteration. But this is ſuch an indulgence, as thoſe faithful and judicious men well knew they had neither a right to grant, nor a liberty to accept of; and if they are permitted to ſpeak for themſelves, they will ſoon be cleared of the accuſation here brought againſt them. For nothing can more expreſsly ſet aſide ſuch a looſe acceptation of their words, or more juſtly characterize all our reforming adventurers, than the lines which immediately follow the above paſſage, extracted from their Preface to the *Book of Common Prayer.* Their obſervation is this, " accordingly
" we find, that in the reigns of ſeveral
" Princes of bleſſed memory ſince the re-
" formation, the church, upon juſt and
" weighty conſiderations, her thereunto
" moving, hath yielded to make ſuch alte-
" rations in *ſome particulars,* as in their re-
" ſpective times were thought convenient:

yet

"yet *so*, as that the *main body* and *essentials* of it (as well in the *chiefest materials*, as in the frame and order thereof) have still continued the same unto this day; and do yet stand firm and unshaken, notwithstanding all the vain attempts, and impetuous assaults made against it, by such men as are *given to change*, and have always discovered a greater regard to their own *private fancies* and interests, than to that duty they owe to the public."
They likewise inform us, that after the restoration, "divers pamphlets were published against the *Book of Common Prayer*, by those who under the usurped powers had made it their business to render the people disaffected thereunto; the old objections were mustered up, with the addition of some new ones, to make the number swell." And that at the time of their review, "of the sundry alterations proposed to them, they rejected all such as were either of dangerous consequence (as *secretly striking at some established doctrine*, or laudable practice of the church of *England*, or indeed of the whole Catholic

"tholic church of *Chrift*) or elfe, of no "confequence at all, but utterly frivolous "and vain."

It might have been as prudent therefore in the author, not to have meddled with this Preface; which is directed throughout againft all fuch changeable minds, " as feek " occafion of cavil, or quarrel againft the " Liturgy of the church."

Every reader who hath confidered the extravagant latitude of his reafonings againft the prefent eftablifhment of the church, will fcarcely believe that he means to ftop at *Arianifm*, when he commends that *freedom of thinking*, which he fuppofes to have been promoted by the legiflature, *not only fince the reformation, but even fince the revolution*[y]: and likewife what fort of principles they are, from whence that air of triumph arifes wherewith he obferves, that the *eyes of mankind have* (of late) *been greatly opened*[z]. If their eyes are opened in fuch a manner, as to make them fee nothing but error inftead of truth, and to know what God is, better than he himfelf

does;

[y] Ded. p. 63.   [z] Ibid.

does; happy would it be for them, if they were still blind. But I have such an opinion of my brethren and countrymen, as to think, that, many of them at least, whatever they *may be* in time to come, are not *yet* persuaded, that knowledge, and wisdom, and judgment, is to be found no where but amongst those who have forgotten their *Catechism*: and, that such a suggestion as this, may now, and always be a *slander* against the greater half of them, is all the harm I wish them.

We are now entering upon the work itself, the *Essay on Spirit*; which, I presume, is so called by the author, because, in the beginning of this work he lays down a short system of metaphysical speculations, concerning the nature and essence of God, the Spirit of the world, or *anima mundi*, the operations and essence of the soul of man, together with the existence and power of angels or created spirits. But before he hath advanced many steps into this system, he strikes into objections against the divinity of *Christ* and the *Holy Spirit*; works up his own metaphysical principles with

with what is revealed in the Old and New Teftament; and then cements the whole together with thofe impure traditions of the *Rabbies*, which originally made the word of God *of none effect*, and were infifted upon by the *Jews*, after their difperfion, on purpofe to deface the doctrines of the primitive Chriftian church.

It is not my intention to confront his fyftem with another of the like nature; in doing which I fhould only *fight as one that beateth the air*; and inftead of fhewing his errors, nothing could hereby be manifefted but my own weaknefs. I fhall therefore meddle with this fyftem no farther than as it interferes with revealed truth; and fhall remark, as I go along, his abufe of Heathen learning, and mifapplication of the holy fcriptures; whence it will appear, that his fpeculations, however new they may be thought, are very ancient, and of *Pagan* original.

If, in the courfe of thefe remarks, I fhould fometimes be obfcure and immethodical, I hope it will be chiefly owing to the author's lefs perfpicuous manner of

treating

treating his subject: for when I peruse his book, I confess myself often puzzled to perceive the connection; and his arguments are frequently so dispersed, that it is no easy matter to collect them. However, that I may the more readily be understood, I shall divide my answer into several chapters: the *first* of which shall comprehend his notions concerning the nature and essence of God, the Spirit of the universe, and the human soul—the *second*, those relating to the existence and power of created spirits—the *third*, his objections against the divinity of the *Son*—the *fourth*, his objections against that of the *Holy Spirit*—the *fifth*, the extent and validity of his conclusion—the *sixth*, his enquiry into the sentiments of the primitive Fathers—the *seventh*, his misapplication of the Heathen *Trinities*—the *eighth* and last, his remarks upon the *Athanasian* and *Nicene* Creeds.

CHAP.

CHAP. I.

In which his notions concerning the nature and essence of God, the Spirit or Instinct of the universe, and the soul of man, are considered.

IT must give us some surprize, to see the first scene of this *essay* open with an *atheist* giving his definition of God. The author tells us, " The opinion of *Spinosa* " was, that there is no other *substance* in " nature but God: that modes cannot sub- " sist, or be conceived, without a substance: " that there is nothing in nature, but " modes and substances: and that there- " fore every thing must be conceived as " subsisting *in God*[a]." By which, if I am so happy as to understand him, he means— that as there is nothing in nature but *modes*, or various modifications of action; and as these *modes* cannot subsist without a *substance*, therefore all the motion or action which appears in nature, must proceed

from

[a] *Essay*, p. 1.—Spin. Op. Posth. Eth. par. I. p. 12.

from the intimate presence of *God's substance*, expanded through the universe. Which opinion of *Spinosa*, hath been supposed to terminate in *atheism*; because it asserts in other words, that the universal substance of *Nature* is *God:* which substance being really nothing more than inanimate matter, and the modes therein observable owing to material or *second* causes, under the direction and influence of the *supreme*; this opinion leaves us without any God at all, except that which all idolaters have allowed, *the creature rather than the Creator.*

How far the author's opinion co-incides with this of *Spinosa*, will appear as we proceed. For according to him, " It may be " asserted that there is in nature but one " self-existent being, subsistence, or sub- " stance, which by way of eminence, may " therefore be called *the substance*, or, figuratively and comparatively speaking, the " *only being, subsistence,* or *substance in na-* " *ture*[b]." As to the first part of this sentence, we grant that there is but one *self-existent*

[b] P. 2.

exiſtent being; but it cannot follow from hence, that there is but one *ſubſiſtence* or *ſubſtance*; becauſe a *ſubſtance* (except when it is improperly uſed for the word *eſſence*) always implies ſomething *material*; whereas a *being* may be either *material or immaterial*. However, to make this ſomewhat plauſible, he " would be underſtood to " mean by theſe three words *(being, ſub-* " *ſiſtence,* and *ſubſtance)* one and the ſame " thing[c]:" that when the words are granted to be ſynonymous, whatever is proved of a *being*, may hold good of a *ſubſtance*. I take notice of this, becauſe, in the next page, the ſcripture is introduced giving its verdict in favour of this opinion. " When " *Moſes* (ſays he) enquired of God, by " what name he ſhould make him known " to the children of *Iſrael,* God ſaid, thus " ſhalt thou ſay—I AM *hath ſent me unto* " *you*—which is rendered by the *Sept.* εγω " ειμι ο ων, *I am he that is,* or that exiſts; " as if, comparatively ſpeaking, there was " no other *being or exiſtence* but God[d]." In this comment, the *eſſay-writer* hath dropt

[c] P. 2.   [d] P. 3.

dropt the words *subsistence* and *substance*, and introduced only those of *being* and *existence:* but as he would be understood to mean the same thing by all of them, we have his own authority for substituting one for the other as we think proper; and then his paraphrase upon εγω ειμι ο ων will be, " I am he that *subsists*; as if there were no " other *substance* but *God.*" He adds, that " from this passage it probably was, that " *Plato* borrowed his notion of the name " of God, when he asserted that the word " εςι, *est*, is solely applicable to the nature " of God. And from him it probably was, " that the word ει, *thou art*, was written on " the door of the *Delphic* temple[e]." But the original text can, I apprehend, afford no room either for this comment, or for introducing these Heathen parallels. It is אהוה אשר אהוה, where the *Hebrew* root of the verb אהוה *I am,* is הוה HOVAH *to be*; from whence is plainly derived the word יהוה *Jehovah,* which when given under a paraphrase, doth not *comparatively* denote the *only being* or *substance*, but strictly and
properly

P. 4.

properly, Him, *which was, and is, and is to come*; and expresses the *self-existence* or *essential eternity* of the divine nature, as distinguished from *created* Beings, which have a beginning *a parte antè*, and a dependent duration *a parte post*.

As for the speculations of *Plato*, &c. concerning their false God, it is impossible to make them square rightly with the inspired appellations of the true; and such authorities being extremely vague and uncertain, will at any rate do the *author*'s cause no service; for it is by no means clear that *Plato asserts that the word* εστι *is* solely *applicable to the divine nature*; since he also asserts, that it is applicable to the essence of the human soul[f]. And moreover, while *Plato* tells us that ο ων (or as he hath it in the neuter gender το ον) is the only Being that *exists*; his scholar *Aristotle* holds, that it is the only Being which is abstracted from existence, or which does *not exist*.

The author next considers God as the *first cause*, and argues thus—" The con-
" sciousness of my own existence necessarily

G " leads

[f] Ωσπερ αυτης (ψυχης) εστιν η ΟΥΣΙΑ, εχουσα την επωνυμιαν την του Ο ΕΣΤΙΝ. Phæd. § 41.

"leads to a *first cause*, which first cause can only be *one*, because two first causes are a contradiction in terms." And this argument is ushered in with the following caution, "I hope I cannot be thought so absurd or so impious, as to imagine that there are more Gods than *one*[g]." But his hope as to this particular, how confidently soever it may be expressed, is not well grounded: for this very *absurdity* and *impiety* is imputed to those of the *Arian* persuasion, and I could never yet find that they were able to clear themselves. The orthodox believe, that the divine *essence* is *one*, and that a plurality of *persons* are comprehended by it. But the *Arians* assert, that the *substance* of God is only *one person:* yet allow at the same time (as they must do, or turn *Deists*) that *Jesus Christ* is *God*. Now two different *substances* make two different *Gods*; and in all this they are so far from maintaining the divine *unity*, that it is hard to say wherein they differ from *Polytheists*. This author hath exceeded them all. He owns very freely (as we shall see

[g] P. 5.

see hereafter) that the name *Jehovah* is applied to the three persons of the Trinity; and, therefore, according to the interpretation of that word, which he himself must allow to be of the same sense with *Exod.* iii. 14. I AM THAT I AM, he must hold three *separate self-existent Beings,* which can differ only in name from *three first causes.* To allow that the only name of God which implies *self-existence* is applied to the *second* and *third* persons of the *Trinity,* and then to argue that they are not *coeternal* with the *first,* is to save the orthodox the trouble of exposing the doctrine of *Arius.*

Now we are upon the subject of *self-existence,* it will be proper to note that *Christ* (on more occasions than one) assumes this characteristic of essential divinity. *Before* Abraham *was* (says he) I AM; describing his own existence by the *permanent present,* expressive of that mode of existence, which can only be conceived of the *supreme* God or *first cause.* The comment of *Lucas Brugensis* upon this expression is—*Non dicit* eram, *sed* SUM, *ut notet constantem ipsius, et immobilem æternitatem*[h].

h See *Pele* in loc.

This comment expresses the natural and obvious sense of the words; and is such as will occur to every reader whose head is not already pre-engaged with sentiments of another kind. The *Socinian* interpretation of this text being a very great curiosity, I shall take the liberty of inserting it, with a few remarks. *Before Abraham was, I am.* John viii. 58. The literal construction of the words leads us to this plain and simple truth, that before *Abraham* was born, or did exist, *Jesus Christ*, who speaks the words, had a being and did exist: consequently, it was no wonder that *Abraham* should have seen him. No, saith *Socinus*, the meaning is this—" πριν Αϐρααμ γενεσθαι, " before *Abram* can be *Abraham*, that is, " the *father of many nations*, Εγω ειμι, I, " saith Jesus, must be the Saviour and light " of the world." So that the words contain a *monition* and a *commination*. The monition is, " that the Jews would believe " him *to be the light and Saviour of the* " *world*, before the Gentiles should be " adopted into the number of *Abraham's* " *children*, and he thereby become *the fa-*
" *ther*

"*ther of many nations.*" The *commination* is not indeed expressed, but it is *implied*; viz. " that if once the Gentiles should be
" admitted into favour, the Jews for their
" infidelity, should be disinherited and
" disowned for ever."

This amazing discovery was made by *Lælius*; and if we believe his nephew *Faustus Socinus,—non sine multis precibus, ipsius Jesu nomine invocato, impetravit ipse**. *Erasmus Johannes* had the effrontery to say of it, *fateor me per omnem vitam meam non magis contortam interpretationem audivisse.* *Faustus*, it seems, had hoped better things of the said *Erasmus Johannes— sperabam te potius fassurum, nullam in vitâ tuâ Scripturæ interpretationem te audivisse, quæ hâc sit aut acutior, aut verior, quæve magis divinum quid sapiat, et a Deo ipso patefactam fuisse præ se ferat. Hoc profecto' affirmare ausim, cum Deus illi viro* (Lælio *scil.) permulta aliis prorsus tunc temporis incognita patefecerit, vix quidquam inter illa omnia esse, quod hâc interpretatione divinius videri queat.* Socin. contra Eras. Johan. p. 505.

---
* *Socin,* contr. *Eutrop.* p. 678.

p. 505. cited by Dr. *Edwards* in his *Preservative against Socinianism*. Part. iv. p. 84. where the reader may see an account at large of its manifold and unparalleled absurdities, all blasphemously fathered upon the spirit of truth. The process made use of in educing this marvellous construction is worth observing. First, the word *Abraham* is perverted from a *proper* name into an *appellative*, so that it doth not denote the *person* of *Abraham*, but the privilege and blessing implied in the *changing* of his name. 2. The word γενεσθαι is altered from denoting the *substantial formation* and *existence* of Abraham; into an accidental capacity, or spiritual mutation, whereby he was *made*, not a *man*, like all others at their *birth*, but an allegorical *father of many nations*. 3. The word ειμι, by which our Saviour expressed his own *real* and *substantial existence*, is made, in like manner, to denote his *office* of Messiah. And lastly, instead of a plain, direct, affirmative proposition, the words are asserted to contain a *monition* and *commination*, of which not one syllable is either expressed or implied, or was ever imagined to be by any human creature till the days of *Lælius Socinus*; who thinking his own private judgment too slender a foundation for all these wonderful things to rest upon, pretended to receive them by immediate revelation from heaven. The union of *heresy* and *enthusiasm* which appears upon this occasion is worthy of admiration: but I must return now to our Author.

Concerning the *first cause*, he affirms, that " every thing which exists besides " that, which way soever it is brought in- " to being, whether it be *begotten*, *ema-* " *nated*, *created*, or *spoken forth*, it must " proceed from, and owe its existence to " the WILL as well as power of that first " cause." There is nothing in the scripture to authorize any such supposition, as this of the Son of God *owing his existence* to the *power* of the *first cause*. For by the application of the name *Jehovah* to him, he is *existence itself:* and the new Testament having taught us, that he is *the Power*, as well as *the Wisdom of God*; then if we admit this author's principles, we shall have the abfurd doctrine, that the *Power of God* is *created* by the *Power of God.* However, to make this appear plaufible, he adds, in a note, the opinion of *Athanafius,* who (as he tells us) " acknowleges " it to be impious to fay that God the " Father was neceffitated to act, even when " he begat the Son; and allows alfo that " neither the Son nor the Holy Spirit are " the firft caufe; but the Father alone, " and that the Son and Holy Spirit were " both caufed[i]." In all this, he ftudioufly avoids the word *creature*; though he takes care to exprefs the fame thing in other words, as the *Arians* always did: for which reafon, *Athanafius* in that very page[k], to part of which the author refers us, thus appeals to his readers—" How manifeft is " their craft and equivocation! for while " they are afhamed to call him *(Chrift)* " the *work of God*, or a *creature*, they de- " vife other modes of fpeech, introducing " the term WILL, and faying, that unlefs " he exifted by the *will* of God, God was " neceffitated to have a Son *againft his will.* " But

[i] *Ibid.*   [k] Vol. I. p 512.

"But (adds he) ye impious men, who "pervert every thing for the fake of your "*herefy*, who pretends to afcribe *neceffity* "to God?" And this is his method of *acknowledging it to be impious to fay, that God the Father was neceffitated to act*; which expreffion, as it ftands together with the context, appears in a light extremely different from what it does in the author's reference to it.

'Tis true, *Athanafius* does fpeak of the Father as a caufe, but not in the author's fenfe of a *firft caufe*. " He *begets* the Son "(faith he) and *fends forth* the Spirit, and "therefore, we call the Father a *caufe*[1];" but ftill he applies the term only to the *begetting* of the Son, and the *proceffion* of the Spirit, both of which are the terms of the fcripture. That the relation between any of the perfons of the Godhead, is the fame as that between the *caufe* and the *effect*, or the *work* and the *maker* of it, is what *Athanafius* conftantly denies: and to fhew that the relation does not fubfift in time but in eternity,

---

[1] Γεννᾷ μὲν τὸν Υἱόν· ἐκπορεύει δὲ κὶ τὸ πνεῦμα τὸ ἅγιον κὶ διὰ τῦτο λέγεται ὁ Πατὴρ αἴτι⊙. V. II. p. 443.

eternity, he uses the *present* tense and not the *past*, as this writer is pleased to do in translating his words.

In the course of his Essay, he hath screwed up the doctrine of an *attractive power in matter* to such a ridiculous height, that the great *Newton*, who generally expressed himself with much caution and reserve, and left his *attraction* open to a physical solution, and to the test of future experiments, would have owed him small thanks for the puerility of his speculations; as I may be allowed to call it without offence. I will extract, from this part of his theory, such passages as will enable us to form a judgment of it.—" When we see a
" stone descend to the ground—the cause
" of that motion must be some *spirit* or
" other—since as *nothing can act where it*
" *is not*, that power whereby any body
" continues in motion, is as much the ef-
" fect of some *concomitant spirit*, as the
" power which first put it in motion [m].—
" The tendency of one body towards ano-
" ther, is from the attractive force of some
" spirit,

[m] P. 9.

"spirit, which attractive power being in proportion to the quantity of matter, makes the difference of weight or gravity in bodies".—"Every particle of active or attractive matter muſt be directed in its motions by ſome *ſpirit, united to that matter*, which may have juſt ſuch a quantity of *intellect* communicated to it by its creator, as will enable it to perform thoſe functions which are aſſigned it, in order to carry on the general œconomy of the univerſe[º]?" The philoſophy of theſe paſſages agrees in part with that of ſome ancient heathens, particularly the *Stoics:* but our author's ſyſtem differs from theirs in two particulars, which cannot be conſidered as improvements. 1. They ſuppoſed the active *ſpirit* reſiding in matter to be only *one*, and called it the *ſoul of the world*; but he hath divided this one into infinitely many. 2. To this ſpirit, as to the human ſoul, they gave a *body*, ſuppoſing it to reſide in æther, air, or fire. But the ſpirits of his ſyſtem do their work without the intervention of any

[n] P. 10. [o] P. 11.

any active material fluid; which is as contrary to the sense of antiquity, as to the result of modern experiments, particularly those of electricity.

This intelligent spirit, by which we are to understand the *æther* expanded through the whole solar system, and united to all matter, is the *Athene*, called by *Athenagoras* ἡ φρονησις δια παν]ων διηκεσα, *a mind or intellect pervading all things:* which same *Athene* or *Minerva*, was no other than the active power of the *sun's rays*, or of the æther diffused every way from his orb, as *Macrobius* delivers it from *Porphyry*, who affirmed that *Minerva* was the *power of the sun, which* (besides its wonderful effects upon inanimate bodies) *even communicates prudence and intelligence to the human mind*[p]. The same thing we learn from *Jamblichus*, concerning the *Egyptian* deity, *Neith* or *Neithas*, namely, that it was Θευ ονομα διηκοντ&c. δι ολυ τυ κοσμυ, *the name of a God who pervades all nature*. And *Tatian* accuses the *Greeks* with idolatry, for worshipping —πνευμα δια της υλης διηκον, *a* SPIRIT *which per-*

[p] *Saturn*, Lib. 1. Ch. 17.

pervades matter [q]. But as there is such superabundant evidence to prove that the most ancient heathens assigned the direction of all effects to an *etherial spirit*, endued with *intelligence;* I must not drop the subject, without producing a little more of it. The author of the book *de Diæta* (supposed to be *Hippocrates*, though some think it more ancient) describes this subtile agent under the character of etherial *fire*—" Which silently and imperceptibly
" governs and disposes all nature. In this
" is life, sense, prudence, the power of in-
" crease, motion, diminution, alteration,
" sleep, vigilance; and it doth with an
" incessant activity direct all things both
" in the earth and in the airy regions[r]."
The ancient philosophers, according to *Cicero*, " divided nature into two parts,
" one of which was active the other pas-
" sive." These they subdivided into the
four

---

[q] Orat. cont. Græcos, P 144. Edit. Par.

[r] Πυρ, οπερ παντων επικρατεσιαι, διεπον απαντα κατα φυσιν, αψοφον και οψει και ψαυσει· εν τωω ψυχη, νοω, φρονησις, αυξησις, κινησις, μειωσις, διαλλαξις, υπνος, εγρε γορσις· τετο παντα δια παντος κυβερνα, και τα δε και εκεινα, ουδεκοτε ατρεμιζει. Lib. I. Sect. II.

four elements; of which, *air* and *fire* have the power of *moving* and of actuating, while the others, *earth* and *water*, are paſſive and diſpoſed to receive their impreſſions[s]. With all this, the *igneus vigor*[t], or *ſpiritus intus alens*[u] of *Virgil*, and the intellectual *ſpirit* of our author (though, indeed, he does not ſeem to underſtand it) perfectly agree.

And here, if by the way I may be permitted to give my opinion, I cannot but think that the heathen ſages, bating their atheiſtical compliment of *intelligence*, talk very rationally of this powerful agent the *æther*; which, if conſidered as an inferior or *ſecond* cauſe, under the direction of the *ſupreme*, and purſued in this ſenſe, would certainly open a moſt entertaining ſcene of natural philoſophy[w].

We find this *Spirit*, and its operations, traced in brief by the author through the whole

[s] *Acad. Queſt.* Lib. I. Ch. 6.   [t] *Æneid.* VI. 730.
   Ibid. l. 726.

[w] This hath been attempted ſince the former edition of the *Anſwer* to an *Eſſay on Spirit*, in an *Eſſay on the firſt Principles of Natural Philoſophy*, printed for *Robinſon* and *Roberts*; where the Reader may ſee, if he pleaſes, what hath been ſaid upon this ſubject.

whole creation, under the name of *inſtinct*.
"It is by *inſtinct* (ſays this philoſopher)
"that the minuteſt particles of matter at-
"tract or repel each other: it is by *inſtinct*
"that the flower of the field is directed in
"throwing forth its leaves and its flowers,
"and forming its fruit in due ſeaſon: it is
"by *inſtinct* that the birds of the air build
"their neſts; and the beaſts of the field
"provide for themſelves and their young[y]."
All this is no better than an abuſe of
words: for *inſtinct* denotes that faculty in
animals by which they differ from *plants*,
and all other *inanimate* matter. It is true,
the diſtinction in ſome ſpecies of each is
almoſt imperceptible; and ſo it is in ſome
caſes between *inſtinct* and *reaſon*; which
yet are eſſentially different.

The operations and effects of this *inſtinct*
will help us to diſcover what ſort of *agent*
is here diſguiſed under a term never before
applied to it. He obſerves, that it is the
ſame inſtinct, which enables the beaſts,
&c. to provide for themſelves, and the
flower to throw forth its leaves, and form
its fruit: therefore this *inſtinct* is what the
heathens

[y] P. 23.

heathens called the *foul of the world*, and I find it commented upon nearly in the fame words—*Hæc igitur eſt* ANIMÆ MUNDI *natura et dignitas—quæ cælo ignes accendit, aera ac mare luce æſtuque replet atque attollit, terras* ANIMALIBUS PLANTISQUE, *fœcundat, tellurem denique alternâ in ævum vice nunc pruinis, nunc* FLORIBUS VESTIT [z], Or if we have a mind to take it from *Macrobius*, it will be ſtill more expreſs— FLORUM *ſpecies hic* DEUS (SOL ſc.) *inſeminat, progenerat, fovet, nutrit, maturatque* [a]. In like manner according to the true and proper ſenſe of this affair, we read, in the holy ſcripture, of the *precious things put forth by the Moon* [b], and of the *tender graſs*, which ſpringeth up from the earth, *by clear ſhining after rain* [c]. So that the *author*'s account of *inſtinct*, brings us back again to the *Athene* of *Jamblichus*, and the *virtus ſolis* of *Porphry*.

He, moreover, proceeds ſo far as to think that " *all created ſpirits* may owe the " limits of their exiſtence, and the extent of

---

[z] *Vallin. in Boëth.* Lib. 3. p. 144.   [a] Sat. L. 1. c. 17.
[b] *Deut.* xxxiii. 14.   [c] 2 *Sam.* xxiii. 4.

"of their faculties to *matter:* and that the
"same spirit, which when cloathed with
"one set of material organs, is only capa-
"ble of exerting its intelligence in the per-
"forming of attraction and repulsion, and
"when jarring elements meet, *&c.* breaks
"forth in thunder, lightning, and earth-
"quakes *(cælo* IGNES *accendit)* may, when
"united to a different set, of a more delicate
"contexture, be enabled to *think* and *reason*,
"and when agitated with anger, to break
"forth in quarrels, contention, and war[d]."
So that the soul of a *passionate man*, and the
soul of *gunpowder*, are in nature the same;
only the one is *cloathed* with charcoal and
sulphur, the other with flesh and blood;
and the same soul that operates in a whirl-
wind and tears up trees, may afterwards
operate in a tyrant, and tear up kingdoms.

But there is another very shocking consequence which will naturally flow from
this principle; for if the same spirit which
performs only the offices of attraction and
repulsion in inanimate bodies, may, when
united to a different set of organs, be capable

[a] P. 24, 25.

ble of thought and reasoning; then, *vice versâ*, the same spirit, which, when united to the body of a man, is capable of *thought* and *reason*, may, when that set of organs is dissolved, be united to an inanimate body, and be capable of *exerting its intelligence*, only in the performance of *attraction* and *repulsion*; which destroys the true immortality of the soul, introducing us at the same time to the doctrine of *transmigration*, and to all the jargon of the *Egyptians* about the *revolution of the forms*. But God forbid that any man, who professes himself a *Christian* should be *spoiled* himself, and endeavour to *spoil* others, with such *philosophy and vain deceit* as this!

How irreligious and unphilosophical is it to talk of *intellect*[e] in *thunder* and *lightning!* when all these natural operations are performed by the mechanical agency of the air or *æther*, under the direction of God; for so we find them represented in holy writ—נתנו שחקים קול— ÆTHERES *dederunt vocem,*

[e] *Cornelius Agrippa* in his *occult Philosophy* mentions *nine* orders of *Devils*; the sixth of which was called the *powers of the air*; these are very busy in *thunder* and *lightning*, and their prince is called *Mirizim*. See *Le Grand*'s Body of Phil. p. 89. fol.

vocem, as *Pagninus* renders it; or, as the *English* verſion hath it—*The* AIR *thundered, and* THINE *arrows* (the ſhafts of lightning directed by the hand of the Almighty) *went abroad*[f]. There is, in this place, no mention of any *ſpiritual* agency, but that of the *ſupreme Being*; nor of any ſecondary efficients, but the elements of the heaven, which are not intelligent but mechanical cauſes, with vapours, clouds, and other proper materials to work upon.

So likewiſe as to the affair of vegetation; a plant we perceive will not grow without the agency of *air* and *heat*: whereas, if this operation was performed by the active power of any *ſpirit* reſiding in the plant, then it ſhould continue to extract its nutriment from the earth, and to flouriſh without the external agency of any mechanical inſtrument; which is utterly contradicted by experience.

But, to be no longer ſerious upon ſuch a very odd ſubject, let us allow, that there are *ſpirits* or *intelligencies* reſiding in all bodies, wherein we diſcern any active or attractive

[f] *Pſal.* lxxvii. 17.

tractive power; and that we may hear how this philosophy will sound, I shall attempt to account for, in the author's stile, the wonderful effects of the *loadstone*. In the *loadstone* then, there are two poles, one of which *attracts*, the other *repels*; and since a spirit which hath the operation of attraction assigned to it, *always attracts as a necessary agent*[g], and that which hath the operation of *repulsion* assigned to it, *always repels*[h], there must in a loadstone be *two spirits*, sitting back to back upon the two poles, one performing its office of attraction, and pulling the needle towards it, the other that of repulsion, and driving it off. When the poles are inverted, or the attracting one changed (as it may be) into the repelling and *vice versâ*; the two spirits have agreed to change places; and when by *fire* or the stroke of an hammer, either a loadstone or magnetic piece of iron loses its attracting and repelling power, the spirits are both of them driven out, and must endeavour to amuse themselves in some other branch of philosophy.

He

[g] P. 11.   [h] *Ibid.*

He hath likewife philofophifed much on the operations, and on the effence of the human foul; but in his reafonings upon the former, he feems greatly to have miftaken the meaning both of *Plato* and St. *Paul.* For, having obferved, that the human mind is forced to be at the trouble of " comparing the propofitions, which re-
" fult from the agreement or difagreement
" of our ideas, in order to arrive at truth:
" hence it is, says he, that *Plato*[i], fpeaking
" of human abilities in the inveftigation of
" truth, calls it *beholding things in the glafs*
" *of reafon;* which he explains by faying,
" that as thofe who contemplate an eclipfe
" of the fun, *lofe the fight of it,* unlefs they
" are fo careful as to view its reflection in
" water; fo the eye of an human fpirit is
" too weak to find out truth, unlefs it looks
" at it thro' the medium of reafon; which
" St. *Paul* alfo calls[k], *feeing through a glafs*
" *darkly*[l]."

Plato does not here difcourfe about *comparing propofitions,* that is, about (λογισμὸς) *reafoning;* but (λογοι) the *reafons* of terreftrial

[i] In *Phæd.* [k] 1 Cor. xiii. 12. [l] *Effay,* p. 20, 21.

trial things, or things which *are not*; and informs us, that by attending properly to them, we may thence infer the *reasons* of the (ταοντα) *things which really* ARE; as for example, by obferving nature, it appears that no quality can poffibly admit its contrary. *Fire,* the effence of which is *heat,* cannot become *cold,* and yet continue to be *fire;* therefore, the foul, the effence of which is *life,* cannot poffibly admit its contrary, *death.*

As to the fimilitude which *Socrates* makes ufe of, to illuftrate this his plan of enquiry, the author hath deviated as much from the fenfe of the *Greek,* as if he had followed implicitly fome *Latin* or *French* tranflation. For, fays he, " they who contemplate an " eclipfe of the fun, *lofe fight of it,* unlefs " they are fo careful as to view its reflexion " in water;" whereas *Plato* has it thus— " unlefs they view the image of the fun in " water, or fome fuch thing, they *lofe* (not " the *fight of the fun,* but) their *own eye-* "*fight,*" by gazing attentively upon an object brighter than it can bear[m]. That is, the

---

[m] Διαφθειρονται γαρ τα ενιοι τα ομματα, εαν μη εν υδατι η εν τινι τοιυτω σκοπωνται την εικονα αυτυ. Phæd. § 48.

the mind, by contemplating too clofely the τα οντα, and endeavouring by its own internal energy to behold them as they are in themfelves, will be dazzled and ftupified; but by having recourfe to fenfible objects, and reafoning from an analogy in nature, it may contemplate the images of them without being impaired. This is one of the fineft fpeculations in the philofophy of *Plato:* but no man can make much of it, as it ftands reprefented in an *Effay on Spirit*.

Let us next examine whether St. *Paul*, when he fpeaks of *feeing through a glafs darkly*, hath any view to the *comparing of propofitions*. The *Greek* is, βλεπομεν γαρ αρτι δι᾽ εσοπ]ρȣ εν αινιγματι, τοτε δε προσωπον προ͛ προσωπον. *Now* (in this life) *we fee through a glafs* (or *mirror) by an* æenigma; *but then face to face*. Wherein he alludes to the manner in which we are obliged to attain to all our knowledge of things fpiritual or invifible, that is, by ufing the creation as a mirror in which to behold them: *for*, as he obferves in another place, *the invifible things of God are clearly feen from the*

the creation of the world, being underſtood *by the things which are made.* The whole *natural* world, throughout the ſacred oracles, is referred to as a figure of the *ſpiritual;* inſtances of which it would be endleſs to produce: but as my meaning may not be ſufficiently clear and explicit without a few, it may readily be remembered, that the *power* and *glory* of *Chriſt* is ſet forth in the operations of the viſible *light* or *ſun*[n]—his efficacy in *raiſing the dead,* by the *dew* which cauſes the graſs to ſpring forth from the earth[o]—the difference between a corruptible and incorruptible body, by earthly ſubſtances and the lights of the firmament[p]—the efficacy of the *Holy Spirit* in cleanſing and purifying the *ſoul,* by *water* which cleanſeth the *body*[q]—the hidden manna or inviſible *bread of life,* by natural bread, which ſupports the body, *&c. &c.* Here are *viſibles* ſubſtituted all the way inſtead of *inviſibles;* becauſe as all our ideas enter by the ſenſes, it is impoſſible for us to form any notion of the latter, but

[n] Mal. iv. 2. John viii. 12. [o] Iſ. xxvi. 19.
[p] 1 Cor. xv. 38. *& ſeq.* [q] John vii. 38, 39. 1 Cor. vi. 11. Tit. iii. 5.

but by viewing them through the medium of the former.

To reprefent things fpiritual under the figures of things corporeal, is (according to the fcripture ufage of the word) to fpeak by an *ænigma*; and to attend properly to this method of conveying knowledge, is *to underſtand a proverb and the* interpretation *of it, the words of the wiſe and their (αινιγ-ματα) riddles or divine allegories*; wherein one thing obvious to fenfe is expreffed, and another, beyond the reach of fenfe, intended and underſtood.

The whole meaning therefore of St. *Paul*'s expreffion, as I humbly conceive, is this—all fpiritual truths are fituated as it were above or *behind* us, out of our fight; while the *glaſs* of the creation lies *before* us, and therein we fee them by a faint reflexion: but in another life, when the foul ſhall be perfected, and the body glorified, we ſhall then fee them no longer by reflexion, but *face to face*; that is, we ſhall then receive not the reflected but the *direct* rays which iffue forth from them.

But

But we are now going to consider some operations of the soul, infinitely more gross than those of *thinking* and *reasoning:* for, in the author's opinion, "it is the same "wise agent which operates in the *digestion* "*of our food,* and that enables us to put in "execution the directions of our will'," It is not my province to explain the whole process of *digestion,* &c. nor would the compass of this work admit of the attempt: but, I think, the *Chymists* are pretty generally agreed, that though many things contribute to digestion, as the mechanical *trituration* of the aliments in the stomach, the injection of the *bile* and other *menstruums,* yet the principal agent is *fire* or *heat*'; and Dr. *Keil,* in his excellent little compendium of *anatomy,* accounts for this operation by the rarefaction of the air; which amounts to the very same thing: his words are these—"This force (that is, "of the fluids acting in the stomach) is "much augmented by the *impetus* which "the *heat* of the stomach gives to the par- "ticles of the *fluids;* nor does this *heat* promote

'P. 22.   ' See Dr. *Friend*'s Chym. Lect. p. 103.

"promote *digestion* only thus, but likewise by rarefying the *air* contained in the
pores of our food, which bursts its parts
asunder'." *Air* and *fire* are *material* and
mechanical agents: whether they are *wise*
ones or not, I leave my christian readers
to consider carefully before they turn
Heathens: for this was undoubtedly the
opinion of the ancient heathen philosophers, whose opinions are collected by *Ma-
nasseh Ben Israel*—" *Hipparchus* thought
that the soul was composed of *fire*;
*Anaximenes, Anaxagoras, Diogenes, Cy-
nicus,* and *Critias* maintained, that it
was *air*. Others again contended, that
it was a mixture of *air* and *fire*, as *Epi-
curus*. Others affirmed, that it was a
thin *spirit* diffused through the whole
body, as *Hippocrates Cous*. *Heraclitus
Ponticus* said that the soul is *light*"."
With some, or with all of these, the author must concur in sentiment, when he
refers the operations of the material or

animal

' *Anat. abridg'd*, p. 41.   " *De Resur. Mort.* lib. I.
chap. 8.—the same collection, with several additions to the
same purpose, is to be met with in *Macrobius in Somn. Scip.*
lib. I. chap. 14.

animal spirit to the essence of the immortal and immaterial, which is altogether distinct from it.

The *Chevalier Ramsay* is pleased to say, that the *Pythagoreans* " always distinguish-
" ed between the *understanding* or the *pure*
" *spirit,* and the *animal soul* or *etherial*
" *body:* that they considered the one as the
" source of our *thoughts,* the other as the
" *cause of our motions*"." But I could wish that this learned man had been a little more express in his evidence for the truth of this distinction. It is, to be sure, highly rational to suppose that there is an *animal soul* or etherial fluid diffused through the body; and this agent bids the fairest for supplying us with an easy and natural solution of *muscular motion*[x]*:* but after what manner the *will* or *intellectual spirit* makes its impressions upon this, so as to cause it

to

---

[w] *Theol. of the ancients,* p. 40, 41.

[x] Sir *Isaac Newton* was plainly of this opinion, and has a remarkable passage to our purpose—Adjicere jam liceret nonnulla de *spiritu* quodam subtilissimo, cujus vi & actionibus—sensatio omnis excitatur, & membra animalium ad voluntatem moventur, vibrationibus scilicet hujus *spiritus ad cerebrum & a cerebro in musculos propagatis.* Princip. Schol. gen. ad fin.

to exert its influence, muſt always remain a ſecret.

When the *eſſay writer* imputes theſe mechanical operations of the *material ſpirit*, to, what he calls, a *wiſe agent*, he ſeeks to confirm his *hypotheſis* by this vulgar obſervation, that " when the belly is full, the
" bones would be at reſt; which (ſays he)
" ſeems entirely owing to this, that the
" ſpirit being unmoleſted with human co-
" gitations, and its attendance upon our
" will, may be more *at leiſure* to purſue
" thoſe operations, which are immediately
" neceſſary towards our preſervation[y]."
He doth not impute this to any groſs fumes which ariſe from the ſtomach, and oppreſs the *ſenſory:* no; the *ſpirit* is ſo much taken up with its natural functions of *digeſtion, concoction, ſeparation,* &c. that it is too buſy to think or reaſon. He might have added, as a collateral proof, that when a man takes phyſic, and the ſoul is excerciſing its *purgative faculty*, he is then leſs able to ſtudy, read, or meditate: which may be eaſily accounted for upon his principles; though
phyſicians

[y] Ibid.

phyſicians impute this indiſpoſition to a relaxation of the whole frame, which forbids any intenſe application of the bodily organs. I am willing to believe that the author did not mean it as ſuch; but certainly this notion of the rational ſoul, is a branch of *materialiſm;* and agrees with the religion and philoſophy of *Oanini* and *Spinoſa*.

As I have now finiſhed my firſt chapter, I think it neceſſary to obſerve, that this head of the *Eſſay* we have hitherto been upon, is entitled by the author, *The* Doctrine of the Trinity *conſidered in the Light of Nature and Reaſon,* becauſe, unleſs the reader were reminded of it, he might not ſo readily perceive any connection between that ſacred doctrine, and theſe philoſophical ſpeculations.

CHAP.

CHAP. II

The existence and power of created spirits.

"I. THERE seems to be no contra-
"diction (says the author) in sup-
"posing that God might communicate so
"much power to one of his own *creatures*,
"of a more exalted nature than man, as to
"enable him to *create* inferior beings, and
"frame a world of his own[z]." This is
introduced, I presume, in order to prepare
us for conceiving, that *Christ* may be a
Creator, and yet notwithstanding this, be
himself a *creature*; which, in effect, was
the heresy of *Carpocrates*, who affirmed that
angels were the creators of the world[a]. But
by a *Creator*, the *Christian* world hath always understood a *first cause:* and if there
are more *Creators* than *one*, there are more
first causes than one. So that the *author*
hath hereby entangled himself in a contradiction, which, a while ago, he seemed to
hold

[z] P. 271.
[a] Ὁ δε Καρποκρατης Αγγελυς τε κοσμε δημιεργες ειναι φησι. *Athanas.* Orat. II. contr. Arian.

hold in the very utmoſt contempt. And farther, if God may give this power to one creature, becauſe *there is no contradiction in it* (which, by the way, is ſuch a turn of arguing as will run us upon everlaſting ſuppoſitions) then he may, for the ſame reaſon, communicate this power to any or to all of thoſe ſpirits he hath given being to.

II. He goes on—" We cannot ſay, but
" that ſome ſpirits may be furniſhed with
" bodies of ſo delicate a texture, that they
" may *cloathe themſelves with light, as it*
" *were with a garment, may make the clouds*
" *their chariot, and walk upon the wings of*
" *the wind*ᵇ." We have no right to infer any ſuch thing from a deſcription, meant only of the ſupreme God: for to Him it is, that *the Pſalmiſt* in the preceding verſe addreſſes himſelf—*Bleſs the Lord* (את יהוה) *O my Soul: O* LORD *my* GOD, *thou art become exceeding glorious*, &c. As the ſupreme God is moſt indiſputably here denominated by the word *Jehovah*, it argues a great degree of preſumption in the author to rob him of the context, and apply
it

ᵇ P. 28.

it to *created spirits*, without being able, or even attempting, to produce any reason or authority for so doing.

III. And again—" That no worlds, fill-
" ed with intelligent spirits, were created
" till about 6000 years ago; about which
" time, both *reason* and *revelation* agree,
" that this ball of earth began to *revolve*
" about the sun, is a thought unworthy of
" a philosopher^c." *Reason*, to be sure, hath many proofs that the world was created just about 6000 years ago; the first and most striking of which is, that it cannot prove it to have been created at all. For *Aristotle* maintained that it was *eternal*[d]; and even though he had received some obscure account of the world's creation by tradition, absolutely rejected it as absurd and incredible: and *Aristotle* is, I think, allowed to have been a perfect master of *reason*. But how doth revelation agree, that this ball of earth began to *revolve* about the sun? If the author can shew where the scripture intimates the revolution of the earth, he hath an opportunity of clearing up a diffi-

I

^c P. 30.   ^d *Gale*'s Court of the Gent. P. II. B. 6. ch. 1.

a difficulty, as some think it, in the sacred philosophy.

IV. After he has supposed, that a *creature* may be a *Creator*, purely because it is *no contradiction*, he passes on to that rule or dominion over the earth, and the several nations of it, with which he imagines the angels to be invested. He begins with borrowing a doctrine from the heathen Poets, and then attempts to reconcile the scripture with it. The *Pagan* notion of this matter, as delivered by the *Essay-writer*, is as follows:—" *Hesiod,* one of the first hea-
" *then* authors extant, supposeth myriads
" of invisible spirits, cloathed in air, at-
" tending upon this terrestrial globe, and
" employed as *angels,* that is, *messengers,*
" between the great God and mankind,
" observing their actions, and reporting
" them to *Jupiter.*" And *Plato* says [*],
" that *Saturn* well knowing there was no
" man who could have absolute empire
" over others, without abandoning himself
" to all kinds of violence and injustice, sub-
" jected the nations to *dæmons* or *intelligent*
" *spirits,* as their lords and governors [f]."

His

[*] Plato de Leg. lib. 4.   [f] P. 32.

His accounts for the moſt part being lame and imperfect, it will be proper to examine more particularly into the nature of theſe dæmons: this done, it will be very clear, that there neither is, nor can be, any reſemblance or ſimilitude between them, and the *miniſtring ſpirits* of the true God, mentioned in holy ſcripture.

Heſiod tells us, that " the race of men " which lived in peace and ſecurity in the " golden age under the reign of *Saturn*, " were, when they died (upon the expira- " tion of that happy age) ordained by the " wiſe counſel of *Jupiter* to be dæmons, " which go to and fro about the earth, " clothed in air, obſerving the good and " evil actions of men [g]." The *dæmons* therefore, or *myriads of inviſible ſpirits*, which *Heſiod* ſuppoſeth, are nothing more than the *departed ſouls* of men; as for their being *angels* or *meſſengers* between the *great god* (that is, the *heathen Jupiter*) and mankind, he ſays nothing about it.

There happens to be a very notable contradiction, as to this affair, between *Plato*

[g] Heſiod. E*ζγ.* lib. I. l. 108, &c.

and *Hesiod:* the one supposing these *dæmons* to have been appointed by *Saturn,* that is, during the time of the *golden age;* because his administration and the *golden age* expired together: the other maintaining, that they were ordained by *Jupiter;* who, as it is well known, did not begin his reign, till he had dethroned his father *Saturn.*

Another account of these beings, given more at large, is to be found in *Apuleius,* which I shall contract into as small a compass, as can conveniently be done, and set it down. " There are certain middle powers
" (between the *gods* and *men)* which are
" divine: these the *Greeks* call *dæmons,* by
" whom, as *Plato* supposes, all the miracles
" of magicians are performed, and the va-
" rious signs, such as appear in the entrails
" of beasts, the flashings of lightning,
" *&c.* by which we foretel future events,
" are regulated; for it is not worth the
" while of the *Dii superi* to condescend to
" such offices as these. They have bodies
" so exactly balanced, that they are neither
" too light nor too heavy; for were they
" too light, they might mount upwards,
" and

" and fly off into the more remote etherial
" spaces; were they too heavy, they might
" then be precipitated into the infernal
" regions." The argument made use of by
Apuleius to prove the existence of these
airy *dæmons*, is something curious: " For
" as there are animals which inhabit the
" *earth*, others which live in *water*, and
" others again, as *Aristotle* contends, in
" *fire*; therefore, argues he, it is absurd to
" suppose that the element of *air* is left
" desolate, and without its proper inhabi-
" tants generated in it: as for birds, they
" are more properly to be esteemed ter-
" restrial animals [h]."

Such is the nature of dæmons, as described by the Heathens, who believed in,
and worshipped this tribe, only because
they thought the matter of the universe to
be eternal, and the *air* (of which according to them the human soul was a part)
divine and intelligent. Whether there is
any resemblance between these and the *ministring spirits* mentioned in the *holy scripture*, will appear when we consider, that

[h] *Apul.* de Deo *Socratis*, p. 62, &c.

the former depend upon the matter of this ſyſtem for their exiſtence, and have their reſidence in the lower region of the air; the latter were in being before it, and dwell in the preſence of [i] God. We ſhould likewiſe remember the promiſe of *Chriſt*, that at the *reſurrection* we ſhall be as the *angels of God which are in heaven*; and if by *heaven* is meant the *material heaven*, or expanſe filled with ſpirits, then our reſidence is to be as theirs is, in the *air*, which is every way impoſſible. For at the laſt day, *the heavens ſhall paſs away with a great noiſe, and the elements ſhall melt with fervent heat; the earth alſo, and the works that are therein, ſhall be burnt up* [k].

V. But we ought to enquire, how the *Heathens* can be qualified to give any evidence worth our notice upon this article? The opinion of the *Eſſay-writer* is, that " the *Greeks*, it is certain, and *Plato* in par-
" ticular, borrowed many of their theolo-
" gical ſentiments from the *Hebrews*; a-
" mong whom this, of a number of inviſi-
" ble ſpirits attending upon this globe of
" earth,

[i] Rev. xii. 7. Dan vii. 10.   [k] 2 Pet. iii 10.

"earth, and prefiding over ftates and king-
"doms, was certainly one[1]." The infinite
difparity between the two accounts of thefe
fpirits, as given, on the one hand, by the
heathen philofophers, and, on the other,
by the fcripture, fhould, I think, feem entirely to preclude any fuch fuppofition. But
what *Hebrews* does the author here mean?
not the modern *Jews*, for they borrowed
from the *Greeks*, and corrupted their own
theology by heathen philofophy. If he
means the *ancient Hebrews*, they muft have
been fo very ancient, that none of their
fentiments are to be found but in the early
parts of the fcripture-hiftory. For the
Greeks received moft of their knowledge,
and indeed all their ancient theology, from
the *Phœnicians*; being defcended from
thofe *Canaanites* which in the time of *Jofhua* inhabited *Afia*, who afterwards were
called *Phœnicians*, and fpread themfelves
from *Afia* into *Africa*, and from thence
into *Greece*, *Italy*, &c.

Hence came that knowledge which the
Greeks had of writing or *letters*, from *Cadmus*,

[1] P, 33.

mus, as they fay, but rather from קדם, CaDoM, the *East* [m], the land of *Canaan*, from whence the *Israelites* had driven them. And this indeed they clearly confefs, by calling this *Cadmus* a *Phœnician*, and their letters Φοινικηϊα, *the Phœnician things* [n], as being abfolutely of *Phœnician* or oriental origin.

All their theological fentiments of this early date, were certainly derived from the *Canaanites*; and the very higheft of them muft founder in that idolatry, by adhering to which, the inhabitants of the land of *Canaan* had filled up the meafure of their iniquities, and were exterminated by the armies of the living God.

As for any fentiments of *Phœnician* theology, borrowed and picked up by *Plato* in his travels, he himfelf is not very clear concerning them. He calls them *Phœnician* and *Syrian fables*, and declares that they were απορητοι, *unfpeakable*, that is, (as the learned *Gale* very judicioufly comments) *be-caufe he neither underftood, nor could exprefs*
the

---
[m] See *Mifcel*. Reflexions upon Mr. *Squire*'s Effays.
[n] *Chifhul*'s Antiq. Afiat. p 99. No. 37, 38.

the mind thereof[o]. Now thefe muft have been either portions of the pure fcripture, or *Jewifh* comments upon the fcripture— if they were the former, the original of them muft be found in the *Bible*; if they were the latter, they were legendary; becaufe ever from the *Babylonifh* captivity, to the coming of *Chrift*, they grew daily more and more ignorant, in proportion as oral tradition prevailed, and the plain word of fcripture was thereby corrupted. In either cafe *Plato* confeffes that he did not underftand them, and therefore not much can be gathered from them. As to the affair of *dæmons* or *intelligent fpirits*, in particular, *Plato* expreffes himfelf fo clearly upon this, and withal fo differently from the fcripture, that we may fairly conclude, that this fentiment was *certainly not borrowed* from thence.

However, upon the whole I will confefs (and it muft be confeffed) that many articles in the theology of the Pagans were originally of *Hebrew*, that is, of *divine* extraction: but then they are fo mangled, fo

metamor-

[o] Vol. I. p. 243.

metamorphofed to the purpofes of heathenifm, and turned into the channel of idolatry, that to think of truly explaining any myfterious doctrine of the fcriptures by thefe ethnic perverfions of it, would be no lefs abfurd, than to fearch for the true fenfe of *Virgil* in Mr. *Cotton*'s *Traveftie*.

VI. We now pafs on to the fcripture itfelf; from whence the author hath extracted feveral paffages, in proof of this his doctrine, of a " number of invifible fpirits at-" tending upon this globe of earth, and " prefiding over ftates and kingdoms:" whether thefe proofs have any relation to the point in hand, will appear upon an examination of them.

1. The firft is, the text of *Deut.* xxxii. 8. as rendered by the LXX—*When the Moft High divided to the nations their inheritance, when he feparated the fons of* Adam, *he fet the bounds of the nations according to the number of the angels of God*[p]. The words which the LXX have moft unaccountably tranflated by αγγελοι Θεȣ, *angels of God*, are

in

[p] P. 33, 34, 35.

in the *Hebrew* original, בני ישראל, *children of Israel,* with which our author is so fair as to acknowledge, that the rendering of the LXX does not *exactly agree.* I need not therefore descend to any critical examination of this matter, till he can shew us either that בני ישראל is equivalent to αἰγελοι θευ, or that the authority of the LXX is superior to that of the *Hebrew* text.

2. The second is the following passage from the Wisdom of the Son of *Sirach—For in the division of the nations of the whole earth, God set a ruler* (or *governing angel,* says the *author) over every people; but* Israel *is the Lord's portion*ᵠ. In the first place, this is an apocryphal book of scripture, which the *church doth not apply to establish any doctrine*ʳ; and in the second place, the original word, which he renders by, *governing angel,* is nothing more than ηγεμε-νο•, *a leader* or *head of a nation*ˢ; and yet,

two

ᵠ *Essay,* p. 34. Eccluf. xvii. 17.   ʳ See *Article* VI.

ˢ Ηγεμων is used *Gen.* xxxvi. near 50 times by the LXX in this sense. And in this very book of *Ecclesiasticus,* the word ηγεμενο• signifies a *master* or *ruler*—not an *angelic* one, because certain moral directions are given him for his behaviour, Ch. xxxii. 1. or, as some copies have it, ch. xxxv. the title of which is—περι ηγεμενων.

two pages after this, he boldly refers to this metaphrafe, as if it were a true and undifputed conftruction.

3. " What adds no fmall weight with him in this affair, is an expreffion made ufe of by St. *Paul, Heb.* ii. 5. where, fpeaking of the fecond coming of our Saviour, in a ftate manifeftly fuperior to angels[t], he fays, *for unto the angels hath he not put in fubjection the world to come, of which we fpeak.* Whence it feems to appear, that it was St. *Paul's* opinion, that this prefent world had been put in fubjection to angels[u]." This is an implication of too great importance to be admitted, unlefs other plain and direct paffages of fcripture fhall appear to coincide with it.

4. " This opinion is confirmed by St. *Jude*—for fays he, Αγγελυς τε τυς μη τηρησαντας την εαυτων αρχην, αλλα απολιποντας το ιδιον οικητηριον, &c. *The an-*
" *gels*

[t] How comes the author to confefs that the ftate of *Chrift* is *manifeftly fuperior to angels?* for we know of no intellectual beings, but *God*, angels, and *men*; and as angels are fuperior to men, and *Chrift* fuperior to both, he muft, according to this conceffion, be *God.*   [u] P. 36.

"*gels which kept not their principalities with*
"*due care, but* neglected their proper pro-
"vinces, he (God) hath reserved in ever-
"lasting chains under darkness." Such is
the author's translation, and he asserts, that
the "*verse ought to be so translated*ʷ."
But a more erroneous translation was never
offered by any man of learning in the
world. 1. He is pleased to render αρχην,
principalities, and οικητηριον, *provinces,* in the
plural, when the original words are both
singular; which makes an essential difference. 2. The word αρχη cannot relate to
any principality which the fallen angels
once had over the earth, and forfeited by
a neglect of their duty; because after their
fall, they still preserve their title of αρχαι
—for, saith St. *Paul, we wrestle not against
flesh and blood, but against principalities,*
αρχας ˣ. 3. The words ιδιον οικητηριον, cannot signify, *their proper province,* that is,
a nation over which an angel had the government, because οικητηριον never signifies
any thing but an *habitation* or *dwelling-
place;* and to render it as the author does,

is

ʷ P. 37.   ˣ Eph. vi. 12.

is as unscholar-like a piece of criticism, as if he had asserted, that when *Strabo* calls *Athens* the σοφων οικητηριον, he means that it was the place, in which *wise men were governing angels*. 4. The dwelling of those angels which St. *Jude* speaks of, could not have been any nations or provinces upon earth, because the angels which fell, fell from *heaven*—*How art thou fallen* from heaven, O Lucifer, *son of the morning*[y]*!* 5. When they were cast down from this their first estate and dwelling, the earth was not created; for the fall of the angels was a circumstance which must have happened before the world; because, as soon as the world was created, there was a fallen spirit ready to tempt and destroy mankind.

So that upon the whole, if he had maintained the very contrary, and asserted, not that angels were degraded from the direction of any provinces upon earth, but that they assumed their proper provinces in consequence of their degradation, he would have been much nearer the truth: for those evil

[y] Isa. xiv. 12.

evil spirits with whom we are in a state of warfare, are called κοσμοκράτορες, *rulers of this world*[z]; and the devil himself is called the *prince of this world*. He is also termed the *prince of the power of the air*; and those evil spirits, the ministers of his subtile and destructive wiles, which hover in that element, like hungry and sharp-sighted birds of prey, are the *Dæmons* the author endeavours to obtrude upon us from the heathens, as beneficent ministers of the Almighty.

5. " The prophet *Daniel* declares, that
" the angel *Gabriel* having touched him and
" spoken to him, said, that he was *come to*
" *make him understand what should befal his*
" *people in the latter days*; and that he
" would have come sooner, but that *the*
" *prince* (or *ruling*, or *governing angel*) *of*
" *the kingdom of* Persia, *withstood him one*
" *and twenty days, till* Michael *one of the*
" *chief princes*, or as the *Hebrew* expresseth
" it, the FIRST PRINCE *came to help him*[a]."
The scripture having taught us that it is possible for men to *withstand God*, and for

the

[z] Eph. vi. 12.   [a] *Essay* p. 45. *Dan.* x. 13.

the spirit of God to *strive with men*, it follows that man may as easily resist the ministration of angels; whence it is unwarrantable to suppose that the prophet *Daniel*, when he speaks of the princes of *Persia* and *Græcia*, means (according to the *author*'s metaphrase) *governing angels*. It is plain, he frequently refers to the then condition of those kingdoms, and prophecies concerning the changes of the *Persian* and *Græcian* empires; wherein, amongst the affairs of other *princes*, he alludes to those of *Alexander* and *Darius Codomannus*[b]; so that if the prophecy of *Daniel* be interpreted throughout according to this new plan, the battle of *Arbela* will appear to have been no other than the battle of the angels; we may, therefore, fairly give up all that he hath advanced upon the prophecy of *Daniel*; but before we dismiss it, it will be proper to obviate what he has offered concerning *Michael one of the chief princes*, or the *first prince:* by which, and by another expression in the same prophecy—MICHAEL *the great*

[b] See *Matthiae* Hist. Quat. Monarch. p. 118, &c. p. 302, &c.

great prince, which ſtandeth for the children of Iſrael—he thinks it is intimated that as inferior angels were appointed to rule over other nations, ſo he was commiſſioned by God to rule over *Iſrael*ᶜ.

He ſuppoſes all along that *Michael* is the ſame perſon with *Chriſt*; and the contrary is not made an article of faith.

There is no evidence throughout the whole ſcripture, for a plurality of archangels: we hear only of one, who is αρχων των αγγελων (for ſuch the word is, when given at length) *the head*, or *ruler of the angels*, he whom the angels were commanded *to worſhip*, as being his creatures and ſervants. And theſe angels, which in the book of *Revelation* are called the *angels* of *Michael*, are likewiſe ſaid to be the angels of *Chriſt*; for, *the Son of Man* (as he himſelf hath aſſured us) *ſhall come, in the glory of the Father, with* ʜɪs *holy angels*ᵈ; and again, *the* Son of Man *ſhall ſend forth*, at the end of the world, ʜɪs *angels*ᵉ. Therefore, as the angels have but *one ruler*, and are ſaid to be the angels of *Michael*, and of the

ᶜ P. 47.　ᵈ Matt. xvi. 27.　ᵉ Ibid. xiii. 41.

the *Son of Man*, it seems to follow, that *Michael* and the *Son of Man* are one and the same person. The same inference will offer itself upon a comparison of the two following texts.—*The Lord himself shall descend from heaven with a shout, with the voice of the archangel,* &c[f]. which voice of the *archangel* is elsewhere said to be *the voice of the Son of Man*—*For the hour is coming, in the which, all they that are in the graves, shall hear* HIS *voice, and come forth*[g].

And thus is this matter rightly understood by the very learned and pious *John Gregory*, where, speaking of that voice, which shall awake the dead, he says, "nor shall it be the voice of a God, and not of a man; it shall be an human voice, for by the *archangel* we are to mean the *Son of Man*, for the hour is coming, &c[h]."

The only passage wherein *Michael* is mentioned under the character of the *archangel*, is to be found in the epistle of St. *Jude*—v. 9.—*Michael the* archangel, *when contending with the devil, he disputed about the*

[f] 1 Thess. iv. 16. [g] John v. 25, 27, 28.
[h] *Posth. Works,* part 2. p. 62.

the body of Moses, durst not (or *was not bold to*) *bring against him a railing accusation, but said, the* Lord *rebuke thee.* Now if we turn to the prophecy of *Zechariah*[1], it will appear, that he who spake these words to the devil, as referred to by St. *Jude,* is there expresly characterised as a person of *Jehovah. And he shewed me,* says the prophet, *Joshua standing before the* ANGEL OF THE LORD, and Satan *standing at his right hand to resist him, and* the Lord *said unto Satan,* the Lord *rebuke thee*; where the word translated, *the Lord,* is in both places *Jehovah.* As *Michael,* therefore, hath that *name* applied to him, which without all controversy denotes *self-existence,* he cannot be a *created angel.* Nothing but an unreasonable prejudice to mere sounds, can dispose us to think, that because he is described as *the archangel* or *prince of the angelic host,* he is therefore of the number with those Beings, of whom he is the *head* and *ruler;* since the very same turn of argument will prove that because *God* is called the *king of kings,* or *Christ the prince of the kings of*

[1] Ch. iii. 12.

the earth[k], he is therefore the chief of *earthly* monarchs, and nothing more.

To what hath been said in relation to this second particular, it may be farther added, that the same host of celestial beings are called, not only the angels of *Michael* and of the *Son of Man*, but also the angels of God the Father[l]: from which inter-community of appropriation, it must necessarily be inferred, that as *Michael* and *Christ* appear from hence to be the same person, so it must also appear, that *Christ* partakes of the same divine essence with God the Father, and is his co-equal in majesty, power, and dominion.

It is in the next place to be shewn, that *Christ* under the names of *Michael*, *Jehovah*, or the *great prince which standeth for the children of* Israel, had not " *the care of* " *that nation assigned to him by the Most* " *High*," as the portion of his inheritance; which proposition is by the *Essay-writer* held in the affirmative[m], and a great part of his work rests upon the supposed truth of it.

But

---

[k] *Rev.* i. 5. Αρχων των βασιλεων της γης.   *Rev.* iii. 5. *Luke* xii. 8. *Heb.* i. 6. [m] See *Essay*, P. 34, 45, 47, 48.

But if *Chrift*, as the guide and protector of the children of *Ifrael*, was himfelf the *Moft High*, it muft carry with it a contradiction to fay, that he had the care of that people *affigned* to him, as the portion of his inheritance, *by* the *Moft High*. St. *Paul* obferves, that fome of the *Ifraelites* were deftroyed in the wildernefs, becaufe they *tempted* CHRIST[n], which the divinely infpired *Pfalmift* expreffes by faying, that they *tempted the* MOST HIGH GOD[o].

And again, it is certain that the kingdom of *Ifrael*, was not, according to the author's fenfe of the thing, affigned to *Chrift* the fecond perfon of the Trinity, as to its guardian angel, becaufe this very fame kingdom is alfo appropriated to the *Holy Spirit:* for the prophet *David* in his *laft* prophetic words, thus defcribes or entitles the divine Perfon, to whom he owed his infpiration— *The* SPIRIT OF THE LORD *fpake by me— the* GOD OF ISRAEL faid, *&c.*

We have now gone through all the arguments by which this *angelic* fyftem of government, invented purely for the fake

[n] 1 *Cor.* x. 9.   [o] Pfal. lxxviii. 56. conf. *Exod.* xvii. 2, 7.

of inserting *Jesus Christ* into the class of created angels, is supported. The author of them thinks they have given him a sufficient warrant for setting down the following conclusion—" It is manifest, that, ac-
" cording to the scriptures of the Old
" Testament," (he should have added " and
" of the New," since two of his arguments out of five are taken from it) "angels were
" appointed to preside over people and na-
" tions *upon earth*ᵖ." Not quite so *manifest*, I think, from the foregoing premisses; the first of which is, a version of the LXX, which strongly favours of traditional *Judaism*, and contradicts the *Hebrew* text. 2. A quotation from an *apocryphal* book, wherein the word ηγυμεν☉ is translated, *governing angel*. 3. An expression of St. *Paul*, relating to the *other world*. 4. The fall of angels *before the world*, alluded to by St. *Jude*. 5. The mention made of *human princes* by the prophet *Daniel*.

ᵖ P. 47.

CHAP.

CHAP. III

His objections against the divinity *of* Christ *answered.*

IT is high time for me to inform my reader that I have hitherto omitted to take notice of the *Jewish* evidence, alledged every now and then by the author in support of his opinions; and evidence in plenty he might have collected from *Jewish* writers, if it were possible, for his opinions to be ten times worse than they really are. If their testimony were of any avail *against* the truth, Dr. *Middleton* would have stood a much fairer chance than he did, for shewing that the whole *law of Moses* was a mere human fiction, artfully framed by a cunning fellow, well versed in the *wisdom of Egypt*, to keep a superstitious and silly people under proper regulations [q].

Our author " chuses to lay before his " reader the opinion of the most sensible " and learned among the *ancient Jews*, as " he

[q] See his quotations from *Josephus* cont. App. and *Philo* de exitu—in his *defence of the Letter*, &c. p. 27, 41.

"he finds it very judiciously collected by "*Eusebius* bishop of *Cæsarea* in *Palestine*, "who must be allowed to be a tolerable "judge, because he lived *amongst them* in "the land of *Judæa*[']." What is it, that we must allow him to be a *tolerable judge of?* that the opinions he hath collected were *really Jewish?* no body denies it. But as *Eusebius* did not flourish till towards the beginning of the fourth century, when the *Jews* had been for three hundred years employed in evading the true sense of the scriptures, in order to baffle and confound the followers of *Jesus;* how can it be expected that their impure comments should breathe the uncorrupt spirit of christianity? These are the men, whom he gravely dignifies, in his title page, with the appellation of *ancient Hebrews,* that is, *modern Jews,* who had endeavoured to their utmost so to infect that air the Christians were to breathe in, as to breed a pestilence amongst them. Nay, the *author* himself, to the utter ruin of his whole scheme, so far as the *Jews* are concerned in it, confesses that

ever

[']P. 40.

ever "since the coming of our Saviour,
"not being willing to abide by the expo-
"sitions given to the Old Testament, they
"ran into numberless absurd contrivances
"of expounding the scriptures according
"to hidden and cabalistical meanings¹."

But these, he observes, were the *more modern Jews*; that is, to use his own words all the *Jews* who lived "since the coming "of our Saviour" were *modern*; and pray then, what sort of *Jews* must those have been, *amongst which* Eusebius *lived?* for if they commenced *absurd* and *modern* upon *our Saviour's coming*, how is it possible for them to be *sensible* and *ancient*, three hundred years after it?

At page 41, we find a quotation from *Eusebius*, which extends nearly throughout three pages, the conclusion of which runs thus—" All the *Hebrew* divines, *after* that " God, who is *over all*, and *after* his first " born Wisdom, pay divine worship to the " third and holy power, which they call " the Holy Spirit." But surely these *Hebrew divines* have no authority for saying,

that

¹ P. 39, 40.

that adoration is to be paid to the firſt-born Wiſdom, AFTER that God who is over all; when a little backwarder in the ſame quotation, they confeſs, that this firſt-begotten of the Father *far exceeds all created Beings?* The plain alternative is this; he is either a *created being*, or the uncreated *God*; but he cannot be a *created being*, becauſe he *far exceeds all created beings*; if ſo, divine worſhip is not to be paid to him *after*, or in ſubordination to the Father, but as the ſcripture ſpeaks, all men are to *honour the Son*, EVEN AS *they honour the Father* *.

Again, he tells us, that " the *Jews* made " a *ſecond eſſence* of the *Logos*, which was " begotten by the *firſt cauſe*; and *Philo* " *Judæus* calls the *Logos* (δευ]ερ۞ ϴε۞) " a *ſecond God*, in whoſe image man was " created¹." It ſeems that *all* the *Hebrew divines* agree in theſe matters, and make the *Logos* a *ſecondary God*, one who is to receive a ſort of divine adoration, inferior to that paid to *God, who is over all*. Now, I have the authority of a *Jew* for affirming, that *all the Hebrew divines* maintain the very contrary,

* John v. 23.   ! P. 43.

contrary, and confefs that the *Logos*, or fecond perfon of the Trinity, under another name, that of the *redeeming angel*, is ftrictly and properly to be efteemed *the very God*. For *rabbi Mofes* thus gives his opinion concerning the divine perfon, who appeared to *Jofhua* under an human fhape, as *captain of the Lord's hoft*: " This angel," fays the above-named *Hebrew* divine, " is the *An-*
" *gel-Redeemer,* who in *Exod*. xxxiii. 14.
" is called the *face of God*; but the *face of*
" *God* fignifies GOD HIMSELF AS ALL IN-
" TERPRETERS confefs; of this fame angel
" it is faid, *my name* (the incommunicable
" name *Jehovah) is in him*[u]."

As there can be no perfect coincidence between the prefent *Jewifh* plan and the *Chriftian*; the only poffible ufe that can be made of their writings is, to extract fuch parts of them as contradict the apoftate fcheme, and to turn their own weapons backward upon themfelves; which defign hath been admirably well executed by *Raymund*

---

[u] Ifte angelus eft *angelus Redemptor*, qui eft *facies Dei*. *Exod*. xxxiii. 14. Atqui *facies Dei* fignificat IPSUM DEUM, ut fatentur OMNES interpretes. De hoc dicitur, *nomen meum in eo eft*.—Cited by *Fagius*, upon *Jofh*. v. 14.

mund Martini, a learned *Spaniard* of the thirteenth century, in his *Pugio Fidei*; who by searching with indefatigable labour into all the machinations of this *Synagogue of Satan*[w], hath displayed that inconsistency which is always to be found in men who have no true principles, and hath confuted them out of their own mouths: which after all doth not shew that their sentiments are of any *authority*, but rather that they are of none at all.

We know, that in the time of our blessed Saviour, the scribes and lawyers among the *Jews*, who ought to have been *instructed* by the sacred oracles, *into the kingdom of God*, had *taken away the key of knowledge*; and it is no where recorded, that from that day to this they ever returned it. Nay, ever from that time forwards, they grew continually worse and worse, as to their knowledge of the holy scripture; which they searched only to pervert; and being actuated by the utmost malice against *Him*, instead of whom they had desired a murderer to be released unto them, fell into as great

[w] Rev. ii. 9. and iii. 9.

great a degree of blindness as those men of *Sodom*, who *wearied themselves to find the door* of the house, with the desperate resolution of affronting the divine persons inclosed within it. And though to us, who enter in by *Christ*, the *way*, the *truth*, and the *life*, the scripture is clear and open; yet to them it is as fast shut and closed, as that den into which the prophet *Daniel* was cast, with a stone laid upon the mouth of it, and sealed with the signet of heaven: nor hath the *purpose* of the king yet been *changed* concerning them.

Whatever therefore *Philo* and his brethren may have been pleased to utter, about the *second cause*, the *most ancient of angels*, the *guardian of Israel*, and the *archangel subsisting with many names*—away with it all; let it return to the place from whence it came; and as a final answer to the author upon this subject, and to caution my reader against that trash of *Judaism*, with which the *Essay on Spirit* hath presented us; let me subjoin that earnest injunction of St. *Paul* to *Timothy*, given at a time, when it may reasonably be supposed there

were

were many and much more antient writings of this fort extant—GIVE NO HEED TO JEWISH FABLES.

We are now to enter upon the *Eſſay-writer*'s objections againſt the divinity of *Chriſt*; moſt of which, inſtead of being found arguments, are miſapplied texts of ſcripture, weak ſurmiſes, and groundleſs aſſertions; but that my work may be the ſhorter and the eaſier, I ſhall firſt beg leave to lay before the reader a few propoſitions, which, I apprehend no *Chriſtian* will, and no man of learning can, diſpute the truth of; deſiring only, that as they are very important, he will give them a ſerious and attentive conſideration.

Prop. I. The name יהוה *Jehovah* doth expreſs abſolute *ſelf-exiſtence*.

Prop. II. There is but ONE *being* or *eſſence*, to which this *name* can be applied— *Hear O Iſrael, Jehovah our God, is* ONE JEHOVAH, *Deut.* vi. 4. which our *Saviour* himſelf affirms to be, the very firſt article of the *firſt of all the commandments*[x].

Prop.

[n] *Mark* xii. 29.

Prop. III. This *name* is applied, *ex concesso*, to *three persons*, the Father, the Son, and the Holy Spirit.

Prop. IV. If so applied, it must denote, that these *three persons* are, after some ineffable manner, really and truly ONE; because, by *Prop.* 2. there is but ONE JEHOVAH.

Prop. V. The fall of mankind was occasioned by an offence against the *supreme God*, not against any *created angel*.

Prop. VI. The salvation of mankind is not to be effected by the union of our nature with *created angels*, but with the *supreme God.*—*God was in Christ reconciling the world to himself.* 2 Cor. v. 19 *.

Prop. VII. We are to be reconciled and united to *him*, by means of *his* union with the

---

* Dr. *Clarke* asserts, that " the word *God* in scripture never signifies a complex notion of *more persons than one.*" In answer to which it would be sufficient to shew that such a *complex notion* is signified by the word *Jehovah*. But the text of this 6th. Prop. shews that the word *God* is applied in the same manner in the gospel; to signify under *one word*, the person of the *Son* who made, and the person of the *Father* who accepted the reconciliation. Whether the scheme of Dr. *Clarke* is not totally overthrown by this single passage, I leave the reader to consider. See *Cath. Doctr.* No. xiv.

the human body of *Chriſt.—There is* one *mediator between God and men, the* MAN, *Chriſt Jeſus.*

Having premiſed thus much, I proceed to the objections:

I. The firſt of which is borrowed from an *apocryphal* book of ſcripture—For " the " wife ſon of *Sirach*, ſays our author, when " ſpeaking of the guardian angel of *Iſrael*, " under the name of *Wiſdom*, ſays, *I came* " *out of the mouth of the Moſt High—He* " *that* MADE *me cauſed me to reſt, and ſaid,* " *let thy dwelling be in Jacob, and thine in-* " *heritance in Iſrael.* He CREATED *me in* " *the beginning, before the world, and I* " *ſhall never fail*, &c⁷."

Upon this he remarks, that this Being muſt be underſtood to have been made and *created*, in the ſame ſenſe as the light, when God ſaid, *let there be light, and there was light*; and immediately after this, ſpeaking by a figure of rhetoric, commonly called *tautology*, he ſays, " it is *likewiſe* to be ob-" ſerved that this angel of *Iſrael* is here de-" clared to have been a *created being*, in
" terms

⁷ P. 50, 51. Ecclus. xxiv. 1—12.

"terms as plain as it is in the power of "language to exprefs." Very true, fo it is, and we would have granted it, without being twice told of it: but on what principles, except thofe of popery, can the author eftablifh, or unfettle any point of faith, from a book, which, with good and fufficient reafons, we hold to be uncanonical? Befides, it muft be noted, that the *Wifdom of Sirach*, as we now have it, is nothing more than a *Greek* tranflation of an *Hebrew* original, in which we have fome reafon to fuppofe that the term *created* was not to be found, becaufe it is not ufed in that paffage of the book of *Proverbs*, of which this is a plain imitation, and from whence the next objection is drawn.

II. For to the afore-mentioned obfervation, it is immediately added—" In the "fame *kind of ftyle* (with the above paffage "from the *fon of Sirach*) it is, that *Solomon*, "fpeaking—in the perfon, and under the "character of *wifdom*, faith, Jehovah *pof-* "*feffed me in the beginning of his ways, be-* "*fore his works of old: I was fet up from* "*everlafting, from the beginning, or ever*

"the

"*the earth was; when there* were no
"depths, I was BROUGHT FORTH, *&c.*'"
The word CREATED was plainly for his
purpose, and, therefore he *first* lays hold of
that; as if the book of *Proverbs* were an
imitation of *the Wisdom of Sirach*, not the
Wisdom of Sirach an imitation of the book
of *Proverbs*.

The *Arians*, in the days of *Athanasius*, laid a great stress upon this passage, in a manner putting the success of their whole cause upon the issue of it. They borrowed their sense of it from the *Septuagint*, which renders the words, יהוה קנני, *The Lord created me*; and descanted upon the word *created*, with as much confidence, as our author does upon the same word, borrowed from the *son of Sirach*[a]: whereas the passage, when read in the original *Hebrew*, or in the *English* version, which rightly translates it, loses all its force, and becomes incapable of such an application.

The

---

[z] P. 52. Prov. viii. 22, *&c.*

[a] The words of *Cornelius a Lapide* upon this occasion are— Hic locus erat *Achilles Arianorum*, quo Christum creaturam esse probarunt, quia hic ἐ dicunt, Deus εκτισε με, *creavit me*.

The primitive Fathers, being many of them under the difadvantage of not underftanding the *Hebrew* of the Old Teftament, applied this paffage to the human nature of *Chrift,* which they fuppofed to be here fpoken of in the fame kind of ftile as where he is faid to be *the Lamb flain from the foundation of the world:* to this purpofe *Athanafius* inftructs us, that *Solomon* " doth not fay, *he created me before his* " *works,* that we fhould receive it as fpoken " of the divinity of the *Logos*; fince it was " the God-man, who (as man) was created " *the beginning*ᵇ *of his ways,* whom he af- " terwards manifefted to us for our falva- " tion." The fame is declared by *Epiphanius,* vol. I. 748. And *Pole* upon this place, referring to *Salmazar,* who has collected their opinions, tells us, that the Fathers unanimoufly applied this paffage to the humanity, or human foul, of the Meffiah. The moft ancient of the *Jews* likewife,

after

ᵇ The original is not בְרֵאשִׁית, *in the beginning,* as our *Englifh* verfion fuppofes it to be, but רֵאשִׁית, *the beginning.* See what St. *Jerom* fays upon the words רֵאשִׁית and αρχη, in his comment on the 7th verfe of *Pfal.* xl. (in him the xxxixth.) Vol. III. p. 130. Ed. *Par.*

after their manner of expressing the thing, held that the *soul of the Messiah* was created before the world: and what is very remarkable, in that little short prologue, which is set down before the description *Wisdom* gives of herself in the book of *Ecclesiasticus*, it is said, *Wisdom shall praise* HERSELF (as *we* render it) but the *Greek* is ψυχην αυτης, *her* SOUL. To this, it may be added, that most of the antient theological writers, in strict agreement with the holy scriptures themselves, have determined, that Christ appeared as *man* to the patriarchs and prophets, long before his incarnation. But the shortest and the safest way to rescue this passage from the hands of the *Arians*, is to construe the *Hebrew* literally.

III. I have laboured hard to give the form of an argument to the next objection, but find the difficulty insurmountable. " *Philo Judæus*," it seems, " observes that " the *archangel with many names*, was also " called by the *name of God*ᶜ:" and then the author proceeds to shew from many

places

ᶜ P. 53.

places of scripture, " that the angel which acted as a guardian-angel to the seed of *Abraham*, and presided over the children of *Israel*, is called *Jehovah*." From whence, he would conclude, I presume, that the name *Jehovah* is applied to a *created angel*. But in all this, I cannot discover where his *medium* of proof lies: *Philo* says, that the *archangel* with many names is called by the *name of God*—we find that the angel, which presided over the children of *Israel*, is called *Jehovah:* these are the author's premises: but as the assertion of *Philo* is of no authority, no doctrine can be drawn from the scripture under such an association.

As for the instances the *author* has offered from the Old Testament, in order to shew, that the same person, who is said to be the *angel of Jehovah*, is likewise mentioned under the direct name of *Jehovah*; before these can be of any service to him, there are two very important questions to be settled: the first is, whether the word *angel*, as applied in the scripture to spiritual and invisible Beings, must necessarily denote a *created Being?* The second is, whether the name *Jehovah*, can be applied to such a being? If both of these questions were determined in the affirmative, he would then have instanced something to the purpose: but to beg them both, and proceed to his instances, is not the practice of a fair or a sound Critic.

I shall therefore not trouble either myself or my reader with the tedious labour of setting all these misapplied instances in their proper light; but observe only, that the word *angel*, as signifying literally^d, *one that is sent*, may, and must be applied to the Second and Third Persons of the ever blessed Trinity; because, according to those offices of *redemption* and *sanctification*, they have mercifully condescended to take upon them in the œconomy of grace, they are both said to be *sent* by the Father^e.

IV. The next objection is taken from that declaration of *Jehovah* to *Moses*, wherein it is asserted, that the *face of Jehovah* could not be *seen*, because, said he, *there shall no man see me and live*. But yet at the same

^d מלאך.   ^e John v. 23.—xiv. 26.

same time we are told that *Jehovah* made *all his goodness to pass before Moses*, and permitted him to behold his *back-parts*, אחרי, which the *author* renders, *what followed him*. From whence he argues, that there must have been *two Jehovahs*, that is, a *visible Jehovah* following the *invisible*[f]. But since, as the fact stands recorded, it is not said that *Moses saw* the face of any *Jehovah*; and as it is not possible that there should be two *Jehovahs*, the one distinct from the other, unless the first article of the first of all the commandments is a contradiction to the rest of the scripture; I pass this over without any farther notice. See Prop. 1, 4.

V. The fifth objection presents us once more with the same impossibility, the existence of two *Jehovahs*. For the author sets down the following passage from the Prophet *Zechariah*——*Sing and rejoice, O daughters of* Zion; *for, lo, I come, and I will dwell in the midst of thee,* saith Jehovah —*and thou shalt know that the* Jehovah of Hosts *hath sent me unto thee*[g]*:* and then observes,

[f] *Ess.* p. 60, 61. Exod. xxxiii. 19, &c.
[g] Zech. ii. 10, 11.

obferves, that " the *Jehovah of Zion* is
" plainly diftinguifhed from the *Jehovah of*
" *Hofts*, and acknowledgeth himfelf to be
" fent by him [h]." It proves, on the contrary, that the *fender* and the *fent*, are effentially *one*. Nor is the *Jehovah of Zion*
diftinguifhed from the *Jehovah of Hofts*;
becaufe, the very perfon, whom the author here fuppofes to be diftinguifhed
from the *fupreme Jehovah*, or God the Father, by the former name, is alfo exprefsly
dignified with the latter. For, faith the
Prophet *Ifaiah*, mine eyes have SEEN the
King, the JEHOVAH OF HOSTS[i], which
when compared with *John* xii. 41. fettles
the point: *Thefe things faid* Efaias, *when he*
SAW *his glory* (the glory of *Chrift*) *and fpake
of him.*

VI. The fixth is not an objection, but a
demonftration againft himfelf; and I cannot conceive what advantage he propofed
in bringing it out to view, for, taking it
as granted that there are two *Jehovahs*, a
fuperior and an inferior, he is pleafed to
obferve hereupon, " that this *Jehovah of*
" *Zion,*

[h] P. 65.   [i] Ifa. vi. 5.

" *Zion*, (whom I have juſt proved to be
" the *Jehovah of Hoſts*) does not always de-
" clare himſelf to be deputed, but actually
" and literally ſpeaks in his own name,
" and calls himſelf *Jehovah*, and ſaith, *I
" am the God of* Abraham; and, *I am the
" God of* Bethel; and, *I brought thee out of
" the land of* Egypt, *&c.* and poſitively
" prohibits *Moſes* and the children of *Iſ-
" rael* from worſhipping any other God
" but himſelf: *thou*, ſays he, *ſhalt have no
" other Gods before me:* thereby ſeeming to
" forbid even the worſhip of the ſupreme
" *Jehovah*, the *Jehovah of Hoſts*[k]." That
is, in other words—when the God, who
brought the children of *Iſrael* out of *Egypt*,
commands them to worſhip him, as the one
only object of adoration, he *ſeems thereby*
to forbid the worſhip of another God *ſu-
perior* to himſelf. No: he thereby forbids
the worſhip of all *inferior* Gods, and af-
ſerts that he himſelf is the *ſupreme:* for the
argument, when drawn up, will ſtand thus
—The *ſupreme God* is to be worſhipped—
but no other God, except him *who brought
the*

[k] P, 66.

the children of Israel *out of* Egypt, is to be worshipped—therefore, the God, who brought the children of *Israel* out of *Egypt* is the *supreme God*. Here the author is under a very grand difficulty, and is far from appearing to be satisfied with his own solution of it[1]. " It is to be observed, says " he, that the *Hebrews* were far from be- " ing explicit and accurate in their stile, " but left great room for the imagination " of the reader to supply and fill up the " deficiencies[m]." And could the author seriously believe, that the *Hebrews*, that is the *Spirit of God* who spake by prophets and holy men amongst the *Hebrews*, hath not an *accuracy in his stile* sufficient to preserve his readers from falling into *Idolatry?* And that the capital doctrine of the Bible is to be settled, not by what *is said*, but by what is *not said?* not by the express words

of

[1] Liquet, veteribus *Judæis* nunquam in mentem venisse commentum illud, quod nostro seculo viris quibusdam doctis inter Christianos placuit; nempe eum, qui *Mosi* in rubo & monte *Sinai* apparuit & locutus est, merum fuisse angelum qui se Deum *Abrahami* appellaret, *Deique nomine* cultum divinum, sibi adhibitum, libenter admitteret. Nimirum absurda nimis, & plane horrenda est illa sententia. *Bulli Def. Fid. Nic.* Sect I. cap. I. § 11. [m] P. 66.

of scripture, but by what the *imagination* is to *supply*? If this were true, such an infallible judge of controversy as the Pope, would seem to be necessary: and therefore the Papists have sometimes been very earnest in objecting to Protestants the ambiguity of the scripture language.

VII. I pass on to the next objection; which is extracted from St. *Paul*[n]: "For, "says this Apostle, *though there be that* "*are called Gods, whether in heaven or in* "*earth (for there be Gods many, and Lords* "*many) yet to us there is but one God, the* "*Father, of whom are all things, and we* "*in him; and one Lord Jesus Christ, by whom* "*are all things, and we by him.* That is, "there is but one supreme God, in com- "parison of whom, there is *none other but* "*he*; and with regard to whom Jesus the "Christ is to be called *Lord*, and not "*God*[o]." In the verse immediately preceding those which are here quoted, the Apostle gives a clear explanation of his meaning, by declaring the very same thing in a few words. *We know*, says he, *that an*

idol

[n] 1 Cor. viii. 5, 6.   [o] P. 87.

idol *is nothing in the world, and that there is no other God but one.* After which, in the words now before us, he draws a contrast more at large, between the belief of *idolaters*, and that of *Christians*, opposing the one only and true God, to that tribe of celestial and terrestrial deities, which by the Heathens were *called Gods*, but, in reality, were nothing in the world. The author imagines, that the Apostle here means to draw a *comparison* between the supreme God, and subordinate angels: for, says he, " the term of *God* is to be attributed to " the Son, as when we say, *there be Gods* " *many.*" But if we say this in the same sense with St. *Paul,* as this writer seems to intend we should, we shall then convert the *Son of God* into an *heathen Idol!* a *nothing in the world!*

It should here be observed, that when the scripture speaks of *one God,* it doth certainly express the *unity* of the blessed Trinity; and the appellation of *the Father,* ascribed to the *one God,* upon which this author and Dr. *Clarke* lay so great a stress, doth not here mean the *person* of the *Fa-*
ther

ther as diftinguifhed from the *Son* and *Holy Spirit*; but denotes, as it does in many other places of the fcripture, the fulnefs of the Godhead which *dwelled bodily* in the perfon of *Chrift*. So he himfelf hath taught us in terms as exprefs as can be defired—*The* Father *that* dwelleth *in me, he doth the works**.

But he carries on this objection in fuch a manner, that we fhall be able to turn his evidence againft himfelf. For this " God " the Father, fays he, St. *Paul* character-" izes as that God, who is *the bleffed and* " ONLY *Potentate, the King of Kings, and* " *Lord of Lords,* WHO ONLY *hath immorta-* " *lity, dwelling in the light which no man can* " *approach unto,* WHOM NO MAN HATH " SEEN, OR CAN SEE^q." This he allows to be a defcription of the *one* only and *fupreme God*; but, it is a defcription of *Chrift*. This is evident, firft, from the context; which, when the connection is preferved, runs thus—*Keep this commandment without fpot, unrebukable, until the appearing of our Lord Jefus Chrift; which he* (the *Lord Jefus Chrift*

---
* John xiv. 10.   ^q Eph. i. 3.   1 Tim. vi. 15, 16.

Chrift himfelf) *fhall fhew, who (Chrift) is the bleffed and only Potentate,* &c. Secondly, becaufe the *appearing* of *Chrift,* here fpoken of, *Chrift* himfelf through the power of the Godhead in him is to manifeft at the end of the world; juft as it is faid of him after his refurrection, *on this wife* SHEWED HE HIMSELF^r. But thirdly and chiefly, becaufe *Chrift* is dignified with all thofe very attributes, which are here afcribed to the fupreme God; and we may take all the articles feparately, and find parallels to them throughout. Firft, *who is the bleffed and only Potentate*—fo of *Chrift* it is elfewhere faid, that he *is the head of all principality and power*^s. 2. *The King of Kings, and Lord of Lords*—fo—*he hath on his vefture and on his thigh a name written,* KING OF KINGS, AND LORD OF LORDS^t. 3. *Who only hath immortality*—fo—*in him was* LIFE^u. 4. *Who dwelleth in the light which no man can approach unto*—fo—*the city* (the heavenly Jerufalem) *had no need of the fun, for the glory of God did lighten it,* and THE LAMB IS THE LIGHT THEREOF^w.

I need

^r John xxi. 1.   ^s Col. ii. 10.   ^t Rev.
^u John i. 4.   ^w Rev. xxi. 23.

I need not run this parallel through the laſt article, the *inviſibility* of the Godhead, becauſe it is to be confidered in a different capacity, as it furniſhes the author with his next objection.

VIII. For, as concerning "the one, only "inviſible God," he affirms very roundly, "that he cannot POSSIBLY be the ſame "with that God, who *was manifeſted in* "*the fleſh*[x]." But by this manifeſtation, none have ever been ſo weak as to imagine, that the *Godhead* became *viſible*, any farther than by its perſonal union with the human nature, which *was* viſible: for when *Chriſt* became incarnate, though we did not ſee *God*, yet we *ſaw* the *perſon who was* God.

Without infiſting afreſh upon that deſcription of *the Father*, (as he will have it) or, *one, only, inviſible God*, which I have juſt now proved applicable to *Chriſt*; I ſhall ſet down two expreſſions, which at once muſt ſilence all cavils and diſputes: for *Chriſt* affirms of the unbelieving *Jews*, that they had both SEEN *and hated, both him and his* FATHER[y]: and again he ſays to one of his

[x] P. 88. 1 Tim. iii. 16.   [y] John xv. 24.

his disciples—*He that hath seen me, hath* SEEN THE FATHER [z]. In both these passages, it is evident to reason and common sense, that the FATHER or *Divine Essence*, could become visible only in respect of his union with the visible person of Christ. And this is such a direct demonstration that the *divine Essence* was actually *so united*, that Dr. *Clarke* and *his myrmidons* [*] never have, nor ever will be able to talk *sense* against it [†].

IX. His next argument runs through 16 of his *sections* [a], in which he hath collected many texts wherein *Christ* is mentioned, as receiving power from God—being *anointed with the oil of gladness above his fellows* (mankind), being *made* Lord and *Christ*—raised from the dead—exalted to the right hand of God, *&c.* all of which relate to the human nature, and cannot possibly afford any evidence for the inferiority of the divine. And let it here be recollected, that the salvation of mankind does not depend upon the exaltation of a God, or of any other

---

[z] John xiv. 2.   [*] See *The Confessional*, p. 316. *first Edit.*
[†] See *Cath. Doctr.* Chap. I. No. 38, and p. 107. 3d *Edit.*
[a] From p. 89, to 106.

other being, but of man only, who fell from God by fin, and through the *man Chrift Jefus*, is re-united to him. It muft be obferved though, that four of the above fections begin with, *and as the Jews,* in which we are obliged with a repetition of that Rabbinical evidence, which hath already received its anfwer, at the beginning of this chapter.

X. " To declare the *Father* and the *Son* " to be *co-equal* and *co-eternal*, is by no " means confiftent with the relation that " there is between father and fon [b]." With that relation, as it fubfifts among *men*, it is not: but this is no reafon, why it fhould not be fo with *God;* or even, that in all created beings it fhould be an inconfiftency. As for example—*Light* is the offspring of *fire*, and yet *co-eval* with it; for it is impoffible to conceive a time, when the fun exifted without emitting light; and were the fun eternal, light would be co-eternal with it: as was very judiciously obferved by

M Mr.

[b] P. 141.

Mr. *Leslie*[c] to the *Unitarians*, many years ago; and it is not answered yet.

XI. "If the substance of the Father be the same undivided substance with the Son, and the substance of the Son became incarnate, then it will follow that the substance of the Father became incarnate also[d]." If the substance of the Father and of the Son were *so united* as not to be distinguished into *two different persons*, this consequence would necessarily follow. But as the scripture doth not teach us, and the church doth not maintain, that the Father and the Son are one person, he hath reasoned upon a false supposition,

[c] Theolog. Works, fol. vol. I. p. 227. I saw this great writer lately mentioned under the name of *that furious high-church bigot* Leslie—the value of which epithets may easily be estimated, if we consider that the vender of them is himself *a furious no-church bigotted Socinian*: for neither the *Socinians* nor the *Quakers* could ever bear the name of Mr. *Leslie*: whose political circumstances being now out of the question, his incomparable skill as a controversialist, acknowledged even by a *Bolingbroke*, ought to recommend his writings to those who would understand the doctrines and interests of the Church of England, in opposition to the Papists on one hand, and Sectarian Enthusiasts on the other. [d] P. 148.

position, and the doctrine of the incarnation is not chargeable with any such absurdities as this author hath taken great pains to fix upon it.

XII. The last objection I shall take notice of, is drawn from the hypostatical union of the two natures in the person of *Christ*, and is as follows—" If this pro-
" position, says he, be taken for granted,
" which may be found *totidem verbis* in
" the *Athanasian* creed, that *as the reason-*
" *able soul and flesh is one man, so God and*
" *man is one* Christ; and if this other pro-
" position be allowed, which is to be found
" as explicitly in the scriptures, that this
" one *Christ suffered* for the sins of man-
" kind; then it must follow, of conse-
" quence, that *Christ* suffered in his *god-*
" *head*, as well as his humanity; since
" otherwise, it would have been the *man*
" *Jesus*, and not *Jesus* the *Messiah*, or
" *Christ*, that suffered for the sins of men [g]."

Hitherto he hath objected as an *Arian*, and talked about the *most antient of angels*, &c. but now, he is changed on a sudden into

[g] Ibid.

into the character of a *Socinian:* for this very argument hath ever been advanced and infisted upon by them, to prove that *Christ* was nothing more than a mere man; becaufe fay they, if God became an individual perfon with man, God muft have *fuffered*; which it is not poffible for him to do. In anfwer to this, I muft recommend to his confideration the two following texts, and if he can, either under the character of an *Arian*, or a *Socinian*, get clear of them, he may proceed with his objection ——*Herein is the love of* GOD, *that* HE LAID DOWN HIS LIFE *for us**. And again *Feed the church of* GOD *which* HE *hath purchafed with* HIS OWN BLOOD †. It is incumbent upon him therefore, if he believes the divine authority of the holy fcriptures, to fhew us, that thefe paffages do not prove, that the *perfon*, who fuffered for us upon the crofs *as man*, was *God* as well as man [h].

* 1 John iii. 16.   † Acts xx. 28.
[h] *N. B.* Thefe three laft objections are intermixed with his *remarks upon the creeds.*

CHAP.

CHAP. IV.

Objections to the divinity of the Holy Ghost answered.

I. "THE Holy Spirit must be an intelligent agent, separate and distinct from God, because he is said to be *sent* by him: for it is manifest that God cannot send himself; because those terms imply a contradiction[l]." It hath already been proved[k], that the *sender* and the *sent* may be essentially one; and as for the supposed *contradiction* of God's *sending himself*, it arises merely from his begging of the question, that there is but one *person* in the divine essence; but the scripture shews that there are *three*, which takes the contradiction away.

II. His next objection is an inference drawn from the following expression—— *Jehovah and his Spirit*[l]; as if, by the usage of the particle *and*, it must necessarily follow that they are separate and distinct beings,

[l] P. 78. [k] See the preceding chapter, Sect. 5.
[l] Ibid.—Isa. xlviii. 16.

ings. But neither will this obfervation hold any more than the former; for *Chrift* thus expreffes himfelf—*I* AND *my Father are* ONE; where, though the particle *and* may feem to disjoin the Father from the Son, yet the whole fentence exprefsly afferts their union: and St. *John*, fpeaking of the whole three perfons, calls them *the Father, the Word,* AND *the Holy Ghoft,* and yet adds —*and thefe three are* ONE. So likewife, when our Lord commanded his difciples to baptize *in the name of the Father,* AND *of the Son,* AND *of the Holy Ghoft*[m], though he inferts the particle *and,* upon which the author grounds his argument, yet he withal expreffes the *unity* of the Trinity: for tho' *three perfons* are mentioned, he bids them not baptize in the *names,* but (εις το ονομα) in THE NAME; upon which the excellent Bifhop *Andrews* thus comments—" If we " will ftay yet, but a little, at our baptifm " and hearken well; as we hear that the " Holy Ghoft is GOD, fo fhall we that he " is GOD *in Unity.* For there we hear but, " *in nomine,* but of *one name.* Now as the
" *Apoftle*

[m] Matt. xxviii. 19.

" *Apostle* reasoneth (Gal. iii. 16.) *Abrahæ*
" *dictæ sunt promissiones & semini ejus. Non*
" *dicit seminibus, quasi in multis; sed, tan-*
" *quam in uno, semini ejus.* To *Abraham,*
" and his *seed,* were the promises made;
" he saith not to the *seeds* as of *many,* but
" to his *seed,* as of one. So we are baptiz-
" ed, *non in nominibus, quasi multis; sed*
" *in nomine, quasi uno;* not in the *names,*
" as of many, but in *the name,* as of one:
" *one name,* and one nature or essence.
" *Unum sumus* (saith *Christ*) of two of them:
" *unum sunt* saith St. *John* of all three;
" this we hear thereⁿ."

III. " In the books of *Judges* and *Sa-*
" *muel,* it is not said, that it was *Jehovah,*
" but the *Spirit of Jehovah,* which came
" upon *Othniel,* and *Gideon,* and *Jeptha,*
" and *Sampson,* and *Saul,* and *David,* to
" assist them in the government of *Israel,*
" and the execution of their office^o." The
last objection was built upon a particle of
three letters; that now before us, hath nothing more to rest upon, than the slender

foun-

⁎ *Sermons,* p. 642.　° *Ibid.* See Judg. iii. 10.—vi. 34,
—ix. 29.—xiii. 25. 1 Sam. x. 6—xvi. 13.

foundation of *two*; for he affirms, it is not said, that it was *Jehovah* himself, but the *Spirit* of *Jehovah*, which inspired and actuated the illustrious persons above-mentioned. But the very first instance he refers us to for a proof of this assertion, shews us, on the contrary, that the same person, who is said to be the *Spirit* of *Jehovah*, is likewise mentioned under the direct name of *Jehovah* himself, which the *author* is pleased to affirm he is not. For of *Othniel* it is said, that *the* SPIRIT OF JEHOVAH *came upon him, and he judged* Israel, *and went out to war; and* JEHOVAH (the same spirit, which enabled him to *go out to war*) *delivered the king of Mesopotamia into his hand.* In like manner, the *Spirit of Jehovah* is asserted to be very *God*, in the passage he refers to concerning *Saul*; for the prophecy of *Samuel* with relation to this matter, is thus worded—*The* SPIRIT of JEHOVAH *will come upon thee, and thou shalt prophesy with them, and shalt be turned into another man: and let it be, when these signs are come unto thee, that thou do as occasion shall serve, for* GOD *is* (or *will be*) *with thee.*

IV.

IV. " St. *John* plainly calleth that *Holy Spirit* by which he was inspired with the book of *Revelations,* an *angel:* for this revelation was signified to St. *John* by an angel sent from *Christ*; and yet through the whole book he calls this revelation the dictates of *the Spirit. He that hath an ear, let him hear what* the Spirit *saith unto the churches*[p]." In this we have a grand specimen of the author's talent in explaining the scripture; for the words here set down, were not spoken by the *angel,* or by St. *John,* but by *Christ* himself, from among *the seven golden candlesticks*[q]. This is a sufficient answer; but I cannot leave this remark without first admitting it to be true, and then tracing a contradiction or two, which must of necessity follow from it. First, if that angel, which signified to St. *John* the scenes described in the book of *Revelations,* was the *Holy Spirit*; then, as it was but one and the same angel of *Jesus Christ*[r], which, from beginning to end, presented all these things before his imagination,

[p] P. 106. Rev. ii. 7. 11. 17.—iii. 6. 13.   [q] *Ibid* i. 13—18, &c.   [r] Chap. i. 1. Ch. ult. 16.

nation, it follows, that the *Holy Spirit* is not to be worshipped; because, when St. *John* offered to pay adoration to the angel, which signified or shewed to him the things he then heard and saw, he was forbid to do it, and at the same time directed to the one only proper object of worship, the supreme God'. Again, as this angel declared to St. *John* that he was his *fellow-servant, and of his brethren the prophets*'; then, if this angel was the *Holy Spirit*, it must appear, that he is a *fellow-servant* with the prophets which he inspired, that is, bound to SERVE or worship the same God: but—all scripture is given by *inspiration* of GOD "—and then, if any thing follows, it is, that *God* is to *worship* himself.

V. " Although the Virgin *Mary* is posi-
" tively said to have been *found with child*
" *of the Holy Spirit*, and to have *conceived*
" *of the Holy Spirit*; yet the person sent to
" her from God upon this occasion, calls
" himself an angel, and in particular, *the*
" *angel* Gabriel *that standeth in the presence*
" *of God*"." The angel *Gabriel* was sent
from

' V. 9.　　' Ibid.　　" 2 Tim. iii, 16.　　" P. 107. Matt. i. 18. 20. Luke i. 19. 26.

from God to forewarn the Virgin of a future efficacy from the *Holy Spirit*, and speaks of the *Holy Spirit* (whom he characterizes as the *Most High*) as of another person; not that he himself was the *Holy Spirit*, as the author imagines, and seems to be so pleased with the discovery, that he thinks it something *very remarkable*.

Now we are upon this subject, I must beg leave to remind him, that *Jesus*, the *holy thing which was born* of the Virgin *Mary* was called the *Son of* GOD, because he was begotten of the *Holy Ghost*; which on more accounts than one, deserves his very serious consideration, and he would do well to clear it up. The very same truth may be collected from many other passages of holy writ; but the following instance may be sufficient—GOD, *who at sundry times, and in divers manners, spake in time past unto the Fathers by the prophets, hath in these last days spoken unto us by his* SON [x]: which GOD, who spake in time past by the *prophets*, and in the latter days by *his Son*, is by St. *Peter* called the *Holy Ghost*: for says he, *in old*

[x] Heb. i. 1, 2.

old time, holy men of God, the prophets, *fpake as they were moved by the* HOLY GHOST [y].

From all which, it manifeftly appears, as I have already obferved, that the whole undivided godhead, is in the fcripture frequently reprefented as the *Father* of the *man Jefus*, and that the *Holy Spirit*, which begat him of the Virgin, is the very and fupreme God; becaufe the angel *Gabriel* calls *his* power, the *power of the* HIGHEST [z]. Nay, the very *devils* themfelves, could with a *loud voice*, call out upon *Jefus* their conqueror, as the *Son of the moft* HIGH GOD [a]; and here the author introduces what he fuppofes to be a created and fubordinate angel *upon this occafion*.

Now we have gone through all the arguments offered in the *Effay*, with the intent of degrading the Son and Holy Spirit to the rank of created beings; it will be proper to enquire, how the writer of it, in allowing them divine worfhip, can poffibly clear himfelf from the charge of *idolatry*,

[y] 2 Pet. i. 21. conf. Luke i. 68, &c. [z] Luke i. 35.
[a] Matt. v. 7.

try, which the *Arians*, upon their principles, have never yet been able to do? Why, he confesses " that angels, as angels, " have no right to divine worship or ado- " ration on their own account; but when " angels are commissioned from God, with " any degree of power over us" (which they never are, being only *ministring spirits*) " and are sent in his name; then it " cannot be idolatry to pay them a propor- " tionate degree of adoration; because " such adoration or worship not being paid " them on their own account, but on ac- " count of the authority which hath been " delegated to them, terminates in the one " only and supreme God[b]."

Thus the difficulty is solved! we are not guilty of idolatry in paying divine adoration to *creatures*, because in them we worship *God*; which is the very excuse *Bartholomew Malam*[c] gave for himself, when he knelt down and worshipped *George Fox* the Quaker; saying, that he did not worship *George Fox* himself, but *the light in George Fox*; that is, he adored the said *George Fox*, not

upon

[b] P. 82, 83.   [c] Leslie Theol. Works, Vol. ii. p. 619.

upon his own account, as *George Fox,* but as one *commiſſioned from God, with a degree of power over us,* raiſed by the irreſiſtible workings of the Spirit, from the ſtate of a mechanick, to that of an inſpired preacher, *a ſon of thunder* uttering a voice upon *Mount Sion,* from the four winds, and *ſent in the name of God.* If the learned will pardon me, for mentioning the name of *Cicero,* in the ſame page, with that of the moſt illiterate *George Fox;* I think the compliment he makes *Scipio Africanus* pay to *Publius,* "*ſcito te deum eſſe*," proceeded from a like principle with that above-mentioned: ſo that *Bartholomew Malam* did nothing more than ſing *Te Deum* to *George Fox,* as the great *Scipio* did to *Publius,* and as the *Eſſay-writer* would perſuade us we may lawfully do to created beings, our fellow-ſervants. But doth he not perceive, that this method of reaſoning will excuſe all the *ſaint* and *angel* worſhip, profeſſed by the modern and ſuperſtitious members of the church of *Rome,* and hitherto ſo juſtly renounced by Proteſtants? For as oft as they are warmly attacked upon this article,

their

their method is, to secure a retreat in the very distinction here advanced by the author, and as oft as confuted, still to insist upon it, that the incense they offer to created beings, ascends through them to the supreme God, and tends to the abundant increase of his honour and glory.

It is, I apprehend, with a retrospect view to this argument, that the author afterwards delivers his opinion, concerning that right which God himself hath to the worship of his creatures; for the case is stated in such a manner, as seemingly to favour the possibility of a title to adoration in inferior beings. The sentiment is borrowed from Sir *Isaac Newton*, though I would hope that great man never intended to make so bad an use of it, and the whole remark is this—" The worship which is due from " man to God, is on account of the *domi-* " *nion* he hath over him *.—So that the
" Son

---

* That divine worship is due from man to God *only* on account of his *dominion*, is not true; for the service of mankind, according to the testimony of scripture, and the reason of the thing itself, is deduced from the perfections and attributes of the object of worship. We are commanded to

worship

" Son becometh our *God*, not so much on
" account of his having been employed in
" the creation, and *that by him God created*
" *the worlds*, as becaufe all judgment is
" committed to him, this being the great
" *obligation* of all duty[d]."

But, to worſhip God as the *Creator* of the world, is alſo to worſhip him as the ſupreme ruler of it; for the act of creation, and the right of ſupremacy, are inſeparable. *The earth is the* LORD's, ſaith the Pſalmiſt, *and the fulneſs thereof, the world, and they that dwell therein:* to which he immediately

worſhip Him that is *perfect* with *perfection* (1); the *Holy one* with *holineſs* (2), the *mighty* one with *humility* (3); and the *merciful* with *mercy* (4) toward our fellow ſervants. Sir *Iſaac* doth indeed ſuppoſe, that God, as God, is *related* to man only on account of his *dominion*; but the obſervation will not hold. His words are theſe, " dicimus *Deus Iſraelis*—non dicimus " *æternus Iſraelis, infinitus Iſraelis, perfectus Iſraelis* (5)." But God is called in ſcripture the *H ly one of Iſrael*, and the *Mighty one of Iſrael:* and this relation being recognized in ſome of the attributes, no reaſon can be given why it ſhould not obtain equally in the reſt. If 1 Sam. xv. 29. be compared in the *Hebrew* with *Jer.* xv. 18. it will alſo appear that the *eternal one of Iſrael* is the beſt conſtruction of the former text.

[d] P. 100, 101.

(1) Matth. v. 48. (2) Lev. xi. 44, 45. (3) 1 Pet. v. 6. (4) Luke vi. 36. (5) *Newt. Princ.* p. *antepenult*.

ately subjoins the reason, why the LORD hath this dominion over the world and all its inhabitants—*for* (or *because*) *he hath founded it upon the seas, and established it upon the floods*[e]. Were it the *dominion* of God, independent of his power as Creator, which lays us under the obligation of worship, then St. *Paul* when he condemned the idolatry of the *Gentiles*, should have stated their crime differently: But he has blamed them only for worshipping the *creature*, rather than the *Creator*[f]; which plainly shews what it is that entitles God to the adoration of mankind; they are his creatures, and therefore they must adore him.

This principle of *dominion*, if it were rested in, would excuse all the abominable idolatry of the *Pagans*, who paid divine honours to the natural rulers, the sun, moon, stars, *&c.* which God hath appointed to *rule* over the day, and over the night, because they deemed them to be the *Gods which* GOVERN *the world*[g]; and the contest between antient believers and unbelievers,

[e] Pf. xxiv. 1, 2. [f] Rom. i. 25. [g] *Wisdom* xiii. 2.

lievers, always turned upon this point, whether thefe natural *rulers* were felf-exiftent, and had power effential in themfelves, or whether they derived it from a *Creator*, who being fuch, was therefore alone to be *worfhipped*. But there is another capital error in this affertion; for, argues he, " the Son becometh *our God*, becaufe *all judgment is committed unto him.*" Now, as far as all judgment is *committed* to the Son, he is not *our God*; becaufe, as far as all judgment is *committed* to him, he is man; for which reafon St. *Paul* declared to his audience of philofophers at *Athens*, that God *will judge the world by that* MAN (εν ανδρι) *whom he hath ordained*[h] : and he is not *our God* by being *man* only, but by being *Emmanuel*, God *with us*, that is, God incarnate. As far as he is a perfon of the God-head, he hath judgment effentially in himfelf; for *vengeance is mine, I will repay, faith* JEHOVAH[i]. Wherefore, let us turn his arguments which way foever we will, and fet them in what light we pleafe, ftill, every way, nothing but error is to be found

[h] Acts xvii. 31. [i] Rom. xii. 19. from *Deut.* xxxii. 35, 36.

found in them; and, therefore, without purfuing them any farther, I may obviate them all at once, by fubjoining the words of God himfelf, by the prophet *Ifaiah,* in relation to this very article. *Thus faith God the* LORD, HE THAT CREATED *the heavens, and ftretched them out—I am* JEHOVAH, *that is my name, and my glory will I not* GIVE TO ANOTHER, *neither my praife to graven images*[k]. No perfon, but the one *Creator,* can have the glory of being called by the name *Jehovah,* or be entitled to any degree of that praife which is due thereupon: and he who is the fupreme Creator of the univerfe, doth here declare, as full as words can exprefs it, that he will not commiffion any OTHER Being to receive divine adoration, fince this is due only to himfelf—THOU SHALT WORSHIP THE LORD THY GOD, AND HIM ONLY SHALT THOU SERVE[l].

[k] Ifa. xlii. 5, 8.   [l] Matt. iv. 10.

CHAP. V.

Wherein the extent and validity of his Conclusion *is examined.*

HERE we shall have an opportunity of seeing what opinion our author entertains of the merits of his own performance, and the strength of his reasonings; how much his conclusion amounts to, and how much, according to the plan, upon which he has proceeded, it ought to amount to. I shall first set down the whole, as it stands in his book, then divide it into particular articles, and make a separate remark upon each of them. His conclusion is this;

" I apprehend therefore, it is manifestly
" shewed in these papers, that from the
" consideration of the nature of spirit, by
" the light of reason it appears, there can
" be but one God, that is, one supreme in-
" telligent agent; which one God may,
" however, create an infinite series of spi-
" ritual agents, in subordination one to an-
" other; some of which may, by an au-
" thority

" thority communicated to them from the
" fupreme God, act *as Gods*, with regard
" to thofe inferior beings, who are com-
" mitted to their charge. I apprehend it
" likewife appears from the fentiments of
" the *Jews*, as well as from the fcriptures,
" both of the Old and New Teftament, that
" this is the method of government, which
" the Almighty hath been pleafed to pur-
" fue in the œconomy of this univerfe, ftill
" referving to himfelf that incommunica-
" ble quality of *fupreme*, which it would
" be a contradiction to fuppofe him diveft-
" ed of, either with or without his will;
" that is, either by his own confent, or by
" neceffity[m].

ARTICLE I.

" I apprehend, therefore, it is manifeftly
" fhewed in thefe papers, that, from the
" confideration of the nature of fpirit, by
" the light of reafon, it appears"—

Answer.

Nothing, concerning the fpiritual or invifible world, can *really* appear by the light
of

[m] P. 113, 114.

of unaſſiſted human reaſon; which borrowing all its fund of ideas from the ſenſes of the body, is circumſcribed by the objects of the ſenſible world, and hath no poſſible means of obtaining any certain knowledge of *things ſpiritual*. Many things, indeed, may *ſeem* to appear, which, in truth, are nothing but the conceptions of the brain, and have no exiſtence any where elſe *in rerum naturâ*. One ſpeculative diſquiſitor may regulate the ſpiritual world in this manner, and another in that; but ſo long as revelation is out of the queſtion, they can neither ſupport their own ſyſtems, nor confute that of another perſon.

For theſe reaſons, therefore, and others before mentioned, it cannot be expected, that, from this topic of argumentation, any thing *real* or worth our notice ſhould *appear* upon the important ſubject now in hand: and, indeed, to conſider any doctrine by the light of nature and reaſon, when there is that of revelation ready at hand, and profeſſedly giving its aſſiſtance, is every whit as imprudent and abſurd, as for a man to reject day-light, and an open road to travel

vel in, that he may shew his genius by taking a solitary walk amongst bogs and pits in the dark, when it is ten to one but he tumbles headlong into the first that lies in his way.

ARTICLE II.

" There can be but one God, that is, but one supreme intelligent agent."

ANSWER.

By *agent* the author means what we intend express by the word *person:* but the *Essay on Spirit* hath nothing to prove that the *supreme nature* is only *one person*. Dr. *Clarke* indeed assures us, that this is the *first principle of Natural Religion**: which assertion, if it were true, would only shew that *Natural Religion* is the same thing with *Deism*, whose first principles are opposite to the Gospel. But it is a notorious matter of fact, that this unity of person was least known to those who were under the influences of nature. The words of *Cicero* on this subject are well worth observing—*Omnibus innatum est et in animo quasi insculptum, esse D E O S* †. " It is a truth

---

* See Cath. Doctr. Pref. p. 32. Edit. 3.
† Cic. de Nat. D. 2, 4.

" truth innate, and as it were engraven upon the mind, that there are GODS." If it be enquired, what principles are dictated by reason independent of revelation, the testimony of *Cicero* who wrote before the Gospel, and spoke in the simplicity of his heart, is of much better authority than that of Dr. *Clarke*, who wrote after it, and was promoting the ends and interests of a private system.

The *unity* of the *supreme nature* is plainly taught by the sense of the word *Jehovah*, as it stands in that text of *Deuteronomy—Jehovah thy God is* ONE JEHOVAH. But this author, contrary to all others I have yet heard of, whether Jews or Christians, hath advanced the unscriptural and senseless doctrine of *two Jehovahs*, a Jehovah *of Zion*, and a Jehovah *of Hosts* *: and therefore, although it is the greatest of all truths that the supreme nature is but *One*, the author of an *Essay on Spirit* is the only man in the world who hath no right to assert it.

ARTI-

---

* See Chap. 3. § 5. supr.

ARTICLE III.

" Which one God, however, may cre-
" ate an infinite feries of fpiritual agents,
" in fubordination one to another."

ANSWER.

True, God may do this; but unlefs it is proved, that *Chrift* and the *Holy Ghoft* are of this number, no progrefs is made in the argument: why was it not affirmed then that they are *creatures?* for whether this appears or not, we are fure, it was the author's intent that it fhould; and his premifes, if they are found and good, prove a great deal more than he hath thought proper here to fet down in his conclufion.

ARTICLE IV.

" Some of which (created fpirits) may,
" by an authority communicated to them,
" from the fupreme God, act *as Gods*,
" with regard to thofe inferior beings, who
" are committed to their charge."

ANSWER.

It ought to have been—" fome of which, may be dignified with the incommunicable name *Jehovah*, declared to be *fupreme*, and adored as *Creators* of the univerfe; and

and yet after all, be in reality, not *Gods*, but *creatures*." As for their being a kind of *quafi dei*, affuming to themfelves the honour of felf-exiftence, and fuffering divine worfhip to be paid to them, only becaufe they were *fent in the name of God*, it is abfurd and impoffible; for a vicegerent or embaffador is never honoured with the title of the monarch he reprefents, or admitted to fit as his equal upon the throne with him[n].

ARTICLE V.

" I apprehend it, likewife, appears from
" the fentiments of the *Jews*, as well as
" from the fcriptures, both of the Old and
" New Teftament, that this is the method
" of government the Almighty hath been
" pleafed

[n] Nefas eft cogitare, hiftrioniam aliquando exercuiffe angelos, et deum incommunicabile nomen ipfis communicâffe, aut talem reprefentationem, in quâ creaturâ omnia, quæ Dei funt, fibi attribuat. Recte etiam doctiffimus Camero: *fane*, inquit, *patroni clientum perfonas fæpe induunt; at ne fando quidem unquam auditum eft, ullum legatum, cùm principis fui mandata proponit, aliter loqui quam in tertiâ perfonâ*: princeps meus hæc dicit. Cujus rei illuftre teftimonium habemus apud prophetas, apud quos nimirum folennis formula eft, Dicit dominus, &c. *Defenfio Fid. Nicæn.* Sect. 1. Cap. i. § 11.

" pleafed to purfue, in the œconomy of
" this univerfe."

ANSWER.

As for the modern *Jews*, I have fhewed that they are not qualified to give their evidence in relation to this or any other point of *Chriftian* doctrine; and the author himfelf hath entered a difqualification againft them, without attempting to reverfe it. As for the *method of government*, or angelic fyftem of politics here alluded to, if the reader thinks it worth his while to turn back to the page in which I have fummed up the evidence alledged in fupport of it, I dare be anfwerable for his *apprehending* no fuch thing.

ARTICLE VI.

" Still referving to himfelf that incom-
" municable quality of *fupreme*, which it
" would be a contradiction to fuppofe him
" divefted of, &c."

ANSWER.

True, it would be a *contradiction* for the *fupreme* to be divefted of this his incommunicable quality; but the *fupreme nature* may ftill be fupreme without being reduced to

an

an unity of perſon: and our Eſſayiſt muſt reaſon in another manner than he hath done, before he will have any right to conclude, that the *Son* and *Holy Spirit*, by ſubſiſting in the unity of the Divine Nature, muſt thereby diveſt it of its ſupremacy.

Such is this mighty concluſion; in the road to which, we have been entertained with romantic ſpeculations of phyſiology, and perverted texts of ſcripture, cemented together with the *Fables* of *Judaiſm!*

CHAP. VI.

His enquiry into the ſentiments of the Primitive Fathers of the Chriſtian church conſidered.

OUR author having thus ſummed up his doctrine in brief, as he apprehends it manifeſtly to appear from his premiſes, is pleaſed to aſſure us, in the next place, that " if we conſult the opinions of " the Fathers upon this ſubject, for the firſt
" three

" three hundred years after Chrift, we fhall
" find them all univerfally agreeing in the
" afore-mentioned doctrine: as may ap-
" pear by confulting *Juftin Martyr, Athe-*
" *nagoras, Tatian, Irenæus, the Author of*
" *the Recognitions, Tertullian, Clemens Alex-*
" *andrinus, Origen, Gregory Thaumaturgus,*
" *Dionyfius of Alexandria, Lactantius,*
" &c.^o"

The *afore-mentioned doctrine,* which we are to find them *all univerfally agreeing in,* is, that the *Son* and *Holy Spirit* are neither of them really God, but act only *as Gods,* and yet are to receive divine adoration from inferior beings. But where are his *proofs?* they come next; becaufe fomething is to *appear,* upon *confulting* the *Fathers.* No; quite another matter: the thing, it feems, is fo clear, that " it is *needlefs* to produce
" any quotations out of them, as this point
" is plainly given up by three of the moft
" learned perfons of the laft age, which
" are, the judicious Mr. *Chillingworth,* the
" learned bifhop *Bull,* and the difcerning
" Dr. *Cudworth^p.*"

How

^o P. 115.   Ibid.

How the case really stands with these three divines, shall be considered, after I have laid before the reader a much more powerful reason for that pretended *needlessness*, by which this author would excuse himself from the trouble of quoting; which is, that all the Fathers he has mentioned, (one only excepted) are universally against his *afore-mentioned doctrine*. But as the extracts I should make from them, would, if set down in their several originals, be calculated only for the satisfaction of the learned, who may as well turn to the books themselves, I may be excused from increasing the bulk of these papers by giving them at length, and shall therefore only refer to the places at the bottom of the page [q].

And

[q] *Just. Mart.* ad Diogn. Epist. Ed. Par. p. 501. υτος ο αει, &c. Resp. ad Orthod. p. 295. επι τυ θευ, &c.—*Athenag.* p. 10. *ibid.* αλλ' εςιν ο υιος, &c.—*Tatian.* Orat. cont. Græc. p. 145, *ibid. Irenæus.* adv. Hæres. lib. iv. c 11. *Dominus enim noster,* &c. and lib. iii. c. 8. *ipse enim infectus,* &c.—*Author of the Apost. Const.* lib. vii. c. 42. Και εις Κυριον Ιησυν, &c.—*Tertull.* adv. Prax. c. 3. Numerum & dispositionem Trinitatis, &c.—*Clem. Alexand.* Admon. ad Gen. p. 5. and 6. Νυν δι, &c. Pædag. l. i. c. 8. p. 113.—*Origen contr. Cels.* lib. vi. p. 287. οτι γαρ τον αγεητον, &c. and περι αρχων, as cited in *Jerom.* tom ix. p. 121. Nunquam utique in Unitate Trinitatis,

And, not to leave my *English* reader quite in the dark, I shall beg leave here to offer one argument, which of itself is sufficient to shew, that all the most early members of the *Christian* church were universally against *his doctrine*; and such an argument it is, as both the learned and unlearned must immediately perceive the force of.

Lucian, who lived as early as the days of *Adrian* (that is, about the beginning of the second century, two hundred years before the council of *Nice)* and was initiated into the Christian faith, but afterwards apostatized to Paganism; this *Lucian*, I say, in one of his dialogues, wherein the interlocutors make it their business to scoff at the Christian religion, puts the following speech into one of their mouths—Υψιμεδοντα Θεον, μεγαν, αμβροτον, ϒρανιωνα, υιον Πατρ⊙, Πνευμα εκ Πατρ⊙ εκπορευομενον, εν εκ τριων, ϗ εξ εν⊙ τρια. Ταυ]α νομιζε Ζηνα, τον δε ηγϒ Θεον. *The almighty God, great, immortal, and celestial, the Son of the Father, the Spirit*

tis, &c.—*Greg. Thaum.* Ed. Par. p. 1. Τρια; τελεια, &c.— For the opinion of *Dionysius of Alexandria,* see *Athanasius,* tom. i. p. 559. &c. *Ignat.* Ep. ad Smyrn. δοξαζω Ιησϒν Χριϛον τον ΘΕΟΝ.

Spirit proceeding from the Father, ONE *of* THREE, *and* THREE *of* ONE: THESE *you must suppose to be* Jove, THIS *you must esteem as God.* To which another makes answer by way of ridicule—ȣκ οιδα γαρ τι λεγεις· εν τρια, κ̓ τρια εν[*]. *I don't understand what you mean: one is three, and three are one!*

This of *Lucian,* though it is but a jeer yet it is so strongly expressed, as to afford us a direct proof, that the doctrine of a *Trinity in Unity,* was in his time professedly subsisting in the church; for it is not any one particular writer, or two, or three, but the whole body of *Christians,* he here aims at. And therefore, it appears as manifestly, that the doctrine of the Trinity, according to our present sense of it, was then universally professed by the *Christians,* as it does from another expression of the same *Lucian,* that they then universally maintained the *resurrection of the dead:* for he derides them all, as a set of poor creatures who amused themselves with the vain hope of being made totally immortal[t].—*fas est et ab hoste doceri.*

As

---

[*] Lucian. Oper. fol. p. 1121.

[t] Πεπεικασι γαρ αυτȣς οι κακοδαιμονες, το μεν ολον αθανατοι εσεσθαι. De Mort. Peregr.

As for Mr. *Chillingworth*, the author favours us with a pofthumous letter of his, given in his life, as written by *Des Maizeaux*, p. 51. which is an anfwer to a friend, who defired to know what judgment might be made of *Arianifm*, from the fenfe of antiquity. If this letter is genuine, what are we to do? are we to fit ftill and be influenced by the authority of a name? or are we to judge for ourfelves, and lament the inftability of *Mr. Chillingworth*? The latter of thefe being the more rational practice, I fhall take the liberty to remark, that Mr. *Chillingworth* hath grofsly mifreprefented the fenfe of antiquity at the beginning of his letter; and given, not only an unfair, but an injudicious ftate of the cafe, at the end of it. He tells his friend, that " even in *Athanafius*
" himfelf, the greateft adverfary of the
" *(Arian)* doctrine, he may find that the
" eighty Fathers, which condemned *Samo-*
" *fatenus*, affirmed exprefsly—*that the Son*
" *is not of the fame effence with the Father.*
" Which is to contradict formally the
" council of *Nice,* which decreed *the Son*

"*co-essential with the Father.*" The eighty Fathers, who condemned *Paul* of *Samosata*, did not deny that the Son was of the same essence of the Father; neither did they formally contradict the council of *Nice*. This crafty fellow, *Paul*, made a wicked use of the word *homoousios*, and by it endeavoured to run the orthodox upon the contradiction of three ουσιαι, or essences in the Trinity[t]: so that when it is said of these eighty prelates, that they rejected the term *homoousios*, *consubstantial*, we are to understand nothing more, than that they rejected it so far only as *Samosatenus* had abused and perverted it; since it is plain, that, in other words, they retained that very sense of the Trinity, which, by the decree of the *Nicene* council, this term was intended to convey. For in their second synodical epistle, written in regard to this arch-heretic, we find the following words—*Qui autem dicit, confiteri filium Dei esse Deum, non esse aliud quam Duos Deos prædicare, hunc alienum esse ab ecclesiasticâ regulâ arbitramur*[u]. Whosoever shall

---

[t] *Dionysii Alex.* Epist. in *Athanas.* v. I. p. 919.
[u] Cited by *Petavius*, Præf. ad Lib. de Trin. ch. ii. § 1.

shall say, that to confess the Son of God to be very God, is the same with preaching up two distinct Gods, (as the said *Paul* did affirm) *such an one we esteem to have departed from the established doctrine of the church.* Now to affirm, as they here do, that the Father and the Son are not *two Gods,* is to affirm that they are *one.* But this unity must be either an unity of essence, or an unity of person: an unity of person it cannot be; therefore it is an unity of essence. And what is this, but the very sense of *homoousios?* wherefore, Mr. *Chillingworth* (if the letter be really his) hath certainly misrepresented these Fathers; it being manifest, that they and the Bishops of the *Nicene* council were of one and the same opinion; though, as occasion required, they may have expressed themselves differently, having two opposite errors to combat: *Paul,* whose heresy was like that of *Sabellius,* would have reduced the whole Trinity to *one Person,* while the *Arians* were for dividing the Unity into *three Gods.*

But in the conclusion of this letter, he in a manner leaves the *Arians* in possession of

of the field; and that for a very fingular reafon. " Whofoever, fays he, fhall freely
" and impartially confider of this thing,
" and how, on the other fide, the ancient
" Fathers weapons againft the *Arians* are
" in a manner only places of fcripture, and
" thofe now for the moft part difcarded as
" impertinent and unconcluding—he fhall
" not chufe but confefs, or at leaft be very
" inclinable to believe, that the doctrine
" of *Arius* is either a truth, or at leaft no
" damnable herefy."

And what *weapons* would Mr. *Chillingworth* have had them ufe? There can be none fo proper, as *the fword of the Spirit, which is the word of God*; by which we fhall be judged at laft, and confequently ought now to be directed. It was the very weapon *Chrift* himfelf made ufe of againft the devil: and though the *Arians* and *Socinians* have done their utmoft to turn the edge of it, it is ftill fharper than the wooden dagger of human wifdom, and will always be found fo when it is put to the trial. I cannot, therefore, be fo *free* and *impartial*, as to conclude with myfelf, that the doctrine

trine of *Arius* was no damnable herefy, purely becaufe the weapons of the Fathers againſt his followers, were in a manner *only* places of fcripture. Whether they are, as he calls them, *impertinent* and *unconcluding*, is another queſtion; with which, as this learned man hath not been pleafed to mention any of them, we have at prefent no concern. Upon the whole, the fcepticifm of this Epiſtle agrees but too well with the character given of Mr. *Chillingworth* by the earl of *Clarendon*, who knew him intimately, and being ſtrongly poſſeſſed in his favour, cannot be fufpected either of ignorance or malice in his report of him. " He " had fpent all his younger time in difputa- " tion; and had arrived to fo great a maf- " tery, that he was inferior to no man in " thofe fkirmifhes; but he had, with his " notable perfection in this exercife, con- " tracted fuch an irrefolution and habit of " doubting, that by degrees he grew con- " fident of nothing, and a fceptic at leaſt, " in the greateſt myſteries of faith *." If this was the cafe, the private correfpondence

* Clarendon's Life, p. 29.

dence of Mr. *Chillingworth* is of very little authority.

We next proceed to Dr. *Cudworth:* and as for him, the *author* tells us, that " he
" does not only give up the Primitive Fa-
" thers in their expressions, but also in their
" meaning^w." Of which, and of the quotation made from the said *doctor*, I shall take no farther notice, than just to subjoin a little short hint, from a scarce and incomparable work of the learned Dr. *Turner* upon mythology, in which we meet with the following stricture upon the *discerning* Dr. *Cudworth*—" But I wonder how it
" came to pass, that the learned writer of
" the Intellectual System, who seems at
" every turn to be so extravagantly fond of
" a Trinity (notwithstanding, as I have
" proved elsewhere, he hath made it his
" business to undermine and overthrow it)
" should be able to make it out so fully,
" that the *Greeks* and *Romans* had a Trinity,
" though *he himself hath none*[x]."

The

---

[w] *Essay*, p. 120.

[x] *Notes on Mythol.*—I cannot refer to the page, because this book was designed only as a preface to a larger work, and is unpaged.

The third divine, who has *plainly given up this point*, and allowed that *Arianism* hath the testimony of all the ancient Fathers, is Bishop *Bull*; even that same Bishop *Bull*, who hath reconciled the Fathers of the three first centuries with the *Nicene* faith; and undertook this work, because it was the vain boast of the *Arian* party (as still it is, for they are never to be silenced) that the most ancient Fathers of the church were the original advocates and propagaters of their heresy.

From this very work it is, that the author extracts a passage, wherein it is confessed, that "almost all the Fathers, who "lived before the council of *Nice*, in their "manner of explaining the article of the "sacred Trinity, sometimes speak other- "wise, than the *Catholics* do²." But this concession can be of no advantage; because it hath been the attempt of this most learned man to prove, by a complete induction of particulars, that although the *Ante-Nicene* and *Catholic* Fathers do sometimes differ in their words and expressions, they

agree

Ess. p. 119, 120. *Def. Fid. Nic.* Sect. 11. c. 9. §. 22.

agree neverthelefs in *fenfe* and *doctrine:* and the learned Bifhop fucceeded fo well in the attempt as to gain univerfal reputation both with Englifhmen and foreigners: though it is certain, that no prefent fuccefs can fecure a man from the future mifreprefentations of his adverfaries; efpecially if they fhould happen to be of the *mendaciffimum genus hominum*; a character, which the aforefaid Bifhop, for their notorious and repeated forgeries, thought proper to beftow upon the *Arians.*

Before we finifh upon this head, it will not be amifs to recollect, that the *author* in his title-page promifed an *inquiry into the fentiments of the Primitive Fathers of the church.* And what does he think an *inquiry* to be? Is it fomething, in which a man never *inquires* at all? for inftead of turning to any pertinent expreffions in the writings of the Fathers, and obliging his readers with a fair and regular difquifition of them, he rather chufes to borrow a fecondhand opinion from thofe, who for different reafons have turned to them, and made different reports concerning them: having done

done this, he treats us with an imperfect account of their answers. One says, that the doctrine of *Arius* is no damnable heresy, because the weapons of the Fathers, on the contrary side, were *nothing but places of scripture*—another, that he discards even the very *meaning* of the Primitive Fathers—and a third, has written a *folio* to prove the very contrary to what he would make him affirm. And this he is pleased to call (by way of banter to be sure) an *inquiry* into the sentiments of the Primitive Fathers; when, as far as they are concerned he seems only just to have *inquired* what their *names* were, and then makes a rattle with *Athenagoras, Gregory Thaumaturgus*, &c.

CHAP. VII.

His misapplication of the Heathen Trinities.

THIS part of his work is entitled, an *Inquiry* into the doctrine of the Trinity, as maintained by the *Egyptians, Pythagoreans*, and *Platonists*. His design in making

making this inquiry, is to point out a subordination of power in the persons of the *Trinity*; that this doctrine, as maintained by the Heathens before the coming of Christ, may confirm his own notion of the *sacred* Trinity. And he is pleased to conjecture, or rather to affirm for truth, that the reason why the *Platonists*, &c. were so ready to embrace the *Christian* religion, was, the close resemblance between the *Pagan* Trinity in general, or the *Platonic* in particular, and the Trinity as maintained in its pure and genuine sense (with a professed subordination of power in it) by the Primitive *Christians*[a]. All of which is *gratis dictum*: for in the first place, it is clear, that the Primitive *Christians*, where they write like themselves, do not allow a subordination of power; and in this he mistakes the *Arians* for the *Christians*, since it is the original *Arian* Trinity, and not the *Christian*[b], that supposes such an inferiority in the persons of the Godhead. It is likewise clear, that the resemblance between the

[a] P. 122, 123. [b] Μᾶλλον Ἀριανοὶ ἢ Χριστιανοί.
Athan. Ep. ad Afr. Episc.

the *Platonic* and the Christian Trinity, as sometimes loosely commented upon by the early writers of the church, be it more or less, did not proceed from any natural affinity between them, but from that strange leaven of false philosophy, with which several of the Fathers corrupted the purity of the Christian system.

But, to come nearer to the point, we must insist upon it, that our author should *inquire*, what the Pagans originally *meant* by their Trinities, and endeavour to explain, before he applies; for to inquire *after* them, and inquire *into* them, are two very different things: the former any body may do; the latter is attended with some labour and difficulty. And unless he can be sure, that the *Pagans*, when they profess a *Trinity*, mean the very same with that of the Old and New Testament, they cannot be permitted to have any share in the controversy.

The inquiry is opened with the *Egyptian* Trinity, as delivered by *Jamblichus*; and yet our author does not attempt to give any satisfactory reasons for producing it, but

but confesses that he cannot translate it. It is *abstruse, dark,* and *super-intelligible;* and he leaves the translation of it to the " *deis-* " *tical* admirers[c] of the religion of na- " ture[d]." A mighty odd way this: first to put the *Heathen* Trinity upon a level with the *Christian,* then draw it up in battle-array, and sound a trumpet before it, as if it were capable of great atchievements against the doctrine he is at war with; and then, on a sudden, to turn short, and ridicule its contemptible obscurity! This *Egyptian* Trinity I shall transcribe, as the *author* gives it[e]; and, with humble submission, try my hand at a literal *English* translation of it: and though it is one of the dark recesses of Paganism, which cannot be properly searched into without much diligence and attention, more than at present I have either leisure or inclination to bestow upon it, yet I shall beg leave to offer, as they

occur

[c] P. 125.

[d] The principles of which religion are so much admired by the author himself, that he has received them as the most effectual test of the scriptural Trinity. For the beginning of his title page runs thus—*An Essay on Spirit, in which the* Doctrine *of the* Trinity *is considered in the Light of* Nature *and* Reason. [e] P. 123, 124.

occur to me, a few hints toward an explanation of it, and readily submit them to better judgments for improvement and correction.

Προ των οντως οντων, και των ολων αρχων εστι Θεὸς εις, πρώτος και τȣ πρωτȣ Θεȣ και βασιλεως, ακινητος εν μονοτητι της εαυτȣ ενοτητος μενων, ȣτε γαρ νοητον αυτω επιπλεκεται, ȣτε αλλο τι. Παραδειγμα δε ιδρυται τȣ αυτȣ πατρὸς, αυτογονȣ, και μονοπατορος Θεȣ, τȣ οντως αγαθȣ. Μειζον γαρ τι και πρωτον, και πηγη των παντων, και πυθμην των νοȣμενων πρωτων ειδων οντων. Απο δε τȣ ενὸς τȣτȣ, ο αυταρχης Θεὸς εαυτον εξελαμ-ψε· διο και αυτοπατωρ, και αυταρχης. Αρχη γαρ αυτος και Θεὸς Θεων. Μονας εκ τȣ ενὸς, προ ȣσιας, και αρχη της ȣσιας· απ' αυτȣ γαρ η ȣσιοτης και η ȣσια· διο γαρ νοηταρχης προσαγορευεται. Αυται μεν ȣν εισιν αρχαι πρεσβυταται παντων, ας Ερμης προ των αιθεριων και εμπυριων θεων προςατ]ει, και των επȣρανιων.

" Before all things which really ARE,
" and before the beginning of all beings,
" there is one God, prior to the first God,
" and king, remaining immoveable in the
solitude

"solitude of his unity; for neither intel-
"lectuality, nor any thing else, is inter-
"mixt with him. He is the exemplar of
"himself the Father, the self-begotten
"God, the only Father, and the truly-
"good. For he is the greatest and the first,
"the fountain of all things, and the root
"of all primary existent forms. But from
"this one, the self-sufficient God shone
"himself out; for which reason, he is self-
"generated and self-sufficient; for he is
"the beginning, and the God of Gods:
"he is unity produced from one; he is be-
"fore all essence, and is himself the be-
"ginning of essence; because, from him
"are entity and essence: wherefore he is
"called the prince of intelligence, These,
"therefore, are the most ancient principles
"of all things, under which, in the third
"and inferior class, *Hermes* ranks the ethe-
"rial, empyreal, and celestial deities."

This, to be sure, if I have been a faithful interpreter, is most infernal jargon: but if the *Egyptian* sages, who drew it up, intended there should be any sense in it, we shall not be likely to discover this sense, by
coming

coming prepossessed with *christian* (or, in effect, *unchristian)* prejudices, and vainly imagining that Heathens, who *knew not God,* must have been prepossessed with the same notions: for it is a plain and serviceable rule in interpreting any author, not to bring his sense to him, and father an intention upon him which he never dreamt of; but to take it from his own words, and support it by a comparison with the sentiments of those that professed the same doctrines.

It will also be allowed as indisputable, that the Heathens themselves best knew what was intended by their own *super-intelligible* mysteries: for which reason, I dare not attempt the short inquiry I have proposed, without taking *Macrobius,* who, as far as I am able to judge, was the most learned of them all, for my guide and director; and then, though the mist is very thick, I have courage enough to hope, that we shall not quite be lost in it. He tells us, that if we would understand the Heathen theology, we must take with us the following admonition—*Cave æstimes, mi Aviene, poetarum gregem cum de diis fabulantur, non*
ab

*ab adytis plerunque philosophiæ semina mutuari*ᶠ. "When the poets relate their my-
"sterious fables about the gods, take it ge-
"nerally for granted, that the subject-
"matter of these mysteries is borrowed
"from the depths of natural philosophy."
This rule *Macrobius* hath made an excellent use of, in unfolding the mysteries of the *Egyptians*, *Pythagoreans*, and *Platonists*; and if it holds good, it must put us upon searching, not for a spiritual or intellectual, but for a physical Trinity, in that precious stuff I have just now translated. The same direction is given us by *Phurnutus* in his treatise concerning the *Nature of the Gods*. " Be assured of this (says he)
" that the ancients were no ideots, but
" able to understand the nature of the
" world, and very happy in their method
" of philosophising by symbols and fa-
" bles *."

In pursuance therefore of this plan, we will lay it down, that the first God herein mentioned,

---

ᶠ *Saturn*. lib. i. c. 17.

* Πεισθεις δ'ι εχ οι τυχονlες εγενονlo οι παλαιοι, αλλα και συνιεναι την τε κοσμε φυσιν ικανοι, και προς το δια συμβολων και αινιγμαlων φιλοσοφησαι περι αυlης ευεπιφοροι. Edit. Gale, p. 105.

mentioned, is the *chaos* or *first matter*; that the second is *light*, or the *sun*; and the third the *soul of the world*, or vivifying spirit diffused from the sun through the whole system of beings, from the stars and planets, down to men, animals, and plants; and I must beg the reader candidly to suspend his judgment till I have run through the whole.

To proceed then,

Before all things which really are, *and before the beginning of all beings, there is one* God, prior *to the first God and King.*

This, as I have already observed, is the *chaos* or *first matter*, as it subsisted in a boundless uncreated mass from all eternity, till the *melior natura*[g], its own intellectual efficacy, brought it into order; or, as *Sanchoniatho* expresses it, till the *dark air of the chaos fell in love with its own principles*, and caused that mixture, from which all the Gods were generated[h]. This same deity, made of right superintelligible, is sometimes called *incomprehensible darkness*, as by

Damas-

[g] *Ovid Met.* lib. I. l. 17.
[h] Ηράσθη το πνευμα των ιδιων αρχων, και ηγειίο συγκρασι:, &c. *Euseb.* Præp. Evan. lib. i. cap 10.

Damascius—Μια των ολων αρχη σκότος αγνωςον[i], *The only principle of all things, is incomprehensible darkness;* and the *Babylonians*, as the same writer informs us, while they *expressed* divine worship to the other Gods, adored this first and super-existent God, by *passing him over in silence*[k]. In the *Orphic* hymns, *Night* is said to be *the begetter of Gods and men*[l]: at other times the Heathens call this same deity, *Proteus;* which, according to the origination of his name (Πρωτευς) is the *first* God, or *first matter*, which originally subsisted under no form, but was capable of assuming any, according to the infinitely various modifications of matter; and hence the poets, agreeable to their custom of borrowing from the *adyta philosophiæ*, tell us so much of his tricks and transformations. That this *Proteus*, or the *first* matter of the *chaos*, is the very same with that Deity, which is here styled

---

[i] All I mention of *Damascius*, is taken from a manuscript fragment, referred to by the learned Bishop *Cumberland* in his Remarks upon the Hist. of *Sanchoniatho*. See p. 280, &c.

[k] Μιαν των ολων αρχην σιγη παριναι. See also *Plato* de Rep. l. vi. p. 686.

[l] Νυκτα Θεων γενητειραν αεισομαι, ηδε και ανδρων.

styled *the one God*, prior *to the first God and King*, must, I apprehend, be evident from a fragment of *Epicharmus*, the most ancient of all the comic poets, wherein it is affirmed that the *Chaos* is the *first* of all the Gods—ΧαΘ- ΠΡΩΤΟΣ των θεων; nor is it possible there should be any sense in the phrase of, a πρω]Θ- τε πρω]ε, a *prior primo*, a God *before the first*; unless by the first πρω]Θ-, we understand, the self-existent matter of the *chaos*; by the second the *light* or *sun*, the first and greatest ruler of the world, who was formed out of it.

It is farther said of him, that he " re-
" mains immoveable in the solitude of his
" unity." He filled the boundless extent of space [m], had no room left to move into, and therefore was in a motionless state of universal stability, since it was impossible that he should change places with himself. But he is in another sense more properly called *immoveable unity*, that is, because out of this first matter all formed sub-

stances

---

[m] Thus *Sanchoniatho* affirms, that the dark air, and turbid matter of the chaos, was for *a long time infinite, and had no bounds.*—ταυlα δε ειναι απειρα και δια πολυν αιωνα μη εχειν περας. *Ibid.*

ſtances are derived; and while they (the forms) undergo the perpetual viciſſitudes of generation and corruption (or diſſolution) that firſt matter out of which they are framed, ſtill keeps ready to its principles, and remains unalterable.

> Omnia mortali *mutantur lege Creata*
> *At manet incolumis* MUNDUS *ſuaque omnia*
>   *ſervat*;
> *Quæ nec longa dies auget, minuitve ſenec-*
>   *tus:*
> *Nec motus puncto currit, curſuſque fatigat.*
> IDEM *ſemper erit, quoniam ſemper fuit*
>   IDEM;
> *Non alium videre patres, aliumve minores*
> *Aſpicient*; DEUS *eſt, qui non mutatur in*
>   *ævum.*
> Manil. Aſtron. l. i. v. 515.

The *unity*, immutability, and divinity of this firſt matter, is a point of very high antiquity; for it was a principle of *Linus*, that *of the one whole are all things, and all that all things conſtitute the one whole*[a], which is the firſt

---

[a] Εκ παντὸς δὲ τα παντα, και εκ παντων το παν εςι. *Stob.* Eclog. Phyſic.

first and incomprehensible God: and *Diogenes Laertius* affirms the same of *Musæus*, who maintained, like all the rest, that *all things are made of* ONE (the homogeneous and eternal matter of the universe) *and that into this* ONE, *they are again all resolved*[o].
And thus also *Plato*, describing the universe, as consisting of first matter, diversified into all the visible *species*, says, that *the* WHOLE *is* ONE *and* MANY[p]: which agrees with the doctrine of *Ocellus Lucanus*, a philosopher more ancient than *Aristotle*, whose whole design it is to shew, that the world is *divine*, that it always existed, and shall always continue; being subject to no change but a perpetual transformation, which he thus describes—Το δε εξ αμφοτερων αυ]ων, τȣ μεν αει θεον]Ꙩ θειȣ, τȣ δε αει με]αϐαλλον]Ꙩ γεννη]ȣ, κοσμꙨ αρχ εςιν[*]. " The " world is composed of these two things, " a divine

[o] Εξ ινꙨ τα παν]α γινεσθαι, και εις τ'αυτον αναλυεσθαι. Diog. Laer. in proœm. S. 3. This capital article of the Egyptian physico-theology was expressed hieroglyphically by the figure of a serpent, in an orbicular posture, with its tail in its mouth; by which, as *Pierius* observes, they meant to signify, *mundum ex seipso ali, et in se revolvi.* Hierogl. l. 14. p. 102. E.
[p] Παν ειναι εν και πολλα. Plat. in Parmen.
[*] Ocell. Luc. cap. ii. ad fin.

"a divine matter which is ever growing "up or flowing into the forms, and ano- "ther matter so begotten, which is ever "changing from one form to another."

It is added moreover, that *neither intellectuality, nor any thing else is intermixed with him: that he is the exemplar of himself, the Father, the self-begotten God, the only Father, and the truly-good.* From all of which, I can understand nothing more, than that matter was self-originated from all eternity without a Creator: whatever else may be intended by it, is abundantly too deep for my capacity. But when it is said, that "*he is the greatest and the first, the* "FOUNTAIN *of all things, and the* ROOT "*of all primary existent* FORMS;" here, I presume, we have a clear proof, that this first God is nothing more than the formless and universal mass of matter, out of which the *forms* are derived, as from their fountain, and from whence they shoot forth, as the stem, branches, and leaves of a tree do from its ROOT. In which very manner, *Jupiter*, as understood to be the one universal God, comprehending all

other

other deities comprehenfible and incomprehenfible in himfelf, is defcribed by *Orpheus*.

Ζευς πρω[τ]Ⓖ γενετο, Ζευς υςατⒼ αρχικεραυνⒼ,
Ζευς κεφαλη, Ζευς μεσσα, ΔιⒼ δ'εκ παντα
τετοκται,
Ζευς ΠΥΘΜΗΝ γαιης, τε και υρανυ αςεροεντⒼ.   Arift. de mundo.

Jupiter *is the firft and the laft, the head, and the midft;* OUT OF *him all things are fabricated: he is the* ROOT *of earth, and of the ftarry heaven.* By which it is meant, as I humbly conjecture, that he is the *firft*, as having exifted in a dark and incomprehenfible ftate, prior to that of the *forms*; the *middle*, as fubfifting *under* the forms; and the *laft*, as refolved, in the continued round of generation and corruption, into his own firft principles again. Much more might be faid of this dark firft caufe; but we will pafs on to the fecond perfon of this Trinity, whofe origin from the firft is fet forth in the following terms. *But from this* ONE, *the felf-fufficient God fhone himfelf out; for which reason, he is self-generated and self-sufficient.*" The *light*, which is the second God here spoken of, did, according to the Heathen creed, extricate itself by its own power from the bands of original darkness, and arose from the confused mass of earthy, airy, and watery matter. For it is affirmed by *Hesiod* in his *Theogony*, that *Chaos*, the first incomprehensible darkness, begat *Night and Erebus;* that is, the *chaos* turned itself into a male and female power, a sort of *hermaphrodite*, and then begat *æther* or *daylight*[q]; who is elsewhere called Ερως, *Love* or *Cupid*, which sprang forth with golden wings from the *chaos*, and hatched it. The *Egyptians* worshipped this same God, under the name of *Cneph*[r], and asserted him to be *without beginning and without end*[s];

and

---

[q] Ητοι μεν ΠΡΩΤΙΣΤΑ ΧΑΟΣ γενετ'—
Εκ Χαεος δ' Ερεβος τε μελαινα τε Νυξ εγενοντο,
Νυκτος δ' αυτ' Αιθηρ τε και Ημερη εξεγενοντο,
Ους τεκε κυσσαμενη, Ερεβει φιλοτητι μιγεισα.
                Theog. l. 116, &c.

[r] Which is the *Hebrew* word כנף CaNePH, a *wing*, and by this name they meant to imitate the swiftness of the *light* in its progress from the sun, and accordingly they made images of this God, painted of different colours, and *winged*. See *Macrob.* Saturn. lib. i. ch. 19. [s] *Plut.* de If. & Osir.

and yet *Damascius* confesses that *Asclepiades* makes his *Egyptian Cneph* or *Cmephis*, to be begotten out of *sand and water*, the muddy mixture of the *chaos*; from which it must be altogether clear, that this God, though without beginning and without end, could yet be no *spiritual* principle[t]; and if not a spiritual, then a *natural* or *physical* principle, which is the very thing I am contending for.

" *He is the beginning, and the God of Gods*"] which *Cicero* expresses, by calling the *sun*, the—*dux et moderator luminum reliquorum*[u]. " *Unity produced from one: he was before all essence, and is himself the beginning of essence; for from him are entity and essence.*"] What the ΕΝ or ONE is, we have seen already; as for this μονας, or *unity* which arose from him, *Macrobius* says of it (just as it was said of *Cneph*) that it is *without beginning and without end*. He also affirms, that it is the *mind begotten of the first cause*; which *mind*, as we learn from another part of his writings, was nothing else but the *sun*[w]. And this is still farther confirmed,

[t] See *Cumberland*'s Remarks, p. 13, 281. [u] Somn. Scip.
[w] In *Somn. Scip.* lib. i. cap. 6. cap. 20.

confirmed, becaufe the *Affyrians* adored the *fun*, under the very name of *unity*; they called him *Adad*, which is plainly a corruption of the *Hebrew* אחד ACHAD, and *Macrobius* fo explains it; for, fays he, *ejus nominis interpretatio, eft* UNUS [x].

How he could be *before all effence* and be himfelf the *beginning of effence*, may, I think, be underftood by the help of an ancient *Scholion* upon a verfe of *Hefiod*, which fupplies us with a very clear diftinction between *firft matter* and *effence*; according to which, υλη, *firft matter*, is to be confidered as an unwrought mafs of metal; ϖσια, *effence*, as the fame mafs hammered into form and figure [y]. Therefore, the *fun*, as his fubftance from all eternity made a part of the formlefs *chaos*, was *before effence*; as receiving a form and figure, upon his felf-generation from it, he is the firft *effence*, properly fo called. The reafon why it is added, that *from him are entity and effence*, is plainly this; the Heathens efteemed the light or power of the fun, to be the fole efficient

[x] Sat. lib. i. c. 23.
[y] Ὑλη μεν εϛιν ὁ χαλϰος, ουσια δε η διατυπωσις του χαλϰου. See *Dan. Heinfius*'s Edit. p. 239. b.

efficient cause in the formation of all the substances in nature: the matter of them they supposed to have been as eternal as himself; but their growth, form, and figure, proceed entirely from his agency: and the *essence* of any thing (as we have already seen) is constituted by its figuration. As intelligence likewise, according to their philosophy, arises from the form or structure of any particular body, and as this structure is owing to the operation of the sun's power, therefore he is (as also for other reasons [z]) dignified with the attribute of νοηταρχης, the "*prince of intelligence.*"—

Thus much for the first and second persons of this *Egyptian* Trinity: as for the third degree of power, it is supported by the whole tribe of *etherial, empyreal,* and *celestial Gods,* amounting to nothing more than the *dæmons* or divine minds, which animate the stars and planets, and people the wide extent of the airy regions; that is, in short, the *intelligent æther* * itself, expanded

---

[z] See what I cited at p. 93. from the book *De Diæta.*

* Δια το τον αιθερα το ηγεμονικον ειναι τu κοσμu, ο δε λογικον εστι. Phurnut. De N. D. p. 69.

panded from the sun's orb, to the extremities of the system.

As *Egypt* was the grand academy of Paganism, and the other Trinities, the *Pythagorean* and *Platonic,* were in all probability borrowed from that we have already considered, it should seem needless to take any particular notice of them; but as the tracing of this affinity may serve to confirm what hath already been said, I shall spend a few words upon each of them.

The first of the two, is given by *Simplicius* in his comment upon *Aristotle,* out of *Moderatus* the *Pythagorean,* and stands thus [a]. Το μεν πρωτον εν υπερ το ον και πασαν ασιαν αποφαινεται· το δε δευτερον εν οπερ εςι το οντως ον, και νοητον, τα ειδη φησιν ειναι· το δε τριτον, οπερ εςι ψυχικον, μετεχειν τε ενος και των ειδων. *The first one he* (i. e. *Pythagoras) declares to be above being and essence: the second one, which is existence and intelligence, he says, is* THE FORMS : *and that the third one, which is animal, partakes of the first one, and of the forms.*

Nothing, in my humble opinion, can (in so small a compass) more completely
explain

[a] Ff. p. 125. Simpl. *in Phys. Arist.* fol. 50.

explain the *Hermetic* Trinity, in the very fenfe I have underftood it, than this does. Here is a προτον εν, a *firſt one*, declared fuperior to all being and *eſſence*; becaufe, as it hath been remarked above, *being* or *eſſence* arifes from *form*, and firſt matter is *without form*. For the fame reafon, the *ſecond one* is called *eſſence* and *intelligence*; and the very name of, *the forms*, is here applied to him, which furely muſt put the matter out of difpute. From our author's account of this *ſecond God*, it muſt evidently appear, that he was either unable, or unwilling to underſtand what he was about. The original is—Το δευτερον εν, οπερ εςι το οντως ον, και νοητον, τα ειδη φησιν ειναι—which he thus tranſlates—" The fecond one, who " is exiſtence itſelf, and intelligence, is " called IDEA [b]." Τα ειδη, THE FORMS, in the *plural*, is according to him, IDEA (an image) in the *ſingular!* which, if compared with the language and the intent of the original, is neither fenfe nor grammar. He was, perhaps, under fome private apprehenſions,

[b] P. 126. He is pleafed once more to deliver this interpretation at p. 131.

henfions, that if he left this multiform Deity in poffeffion of the fecond place in this *Pythagorean* Trinity, all would be fpoiled; becaufe no man could be fo abfurd as to fufpect a parallel between a God who is infinitely many, and the fecond perfon of the facred Trinity, who is only one.

As for the τρίτον εν, or *third one*, it does not exactly anfwer in expreffion to the *etherial Gods* above-mentioned, but in fenfe amounts to the fame. It is the *foul of the world*, the *animal fpirit* that beftows life, fenfe, and motion, upon all rational, animal, and vegetable beings: and what this is, we have already feen from many authorities (to which ten times as many more might foon be added) in the firft chapter.

The laft in order is the *Platonic* Trinity, which inftead of being more refined than the reft, as, according to the extravagant opinion fome men have conceived of *Plato*, it ought to be, rather feems to confirm the whole, and may, therefore, reafonably encourage us to fuppofe, that we have hit upon the true explanation of them all. *Plato*, fays the author, "in that treatife which
"he

"he entitles *Timæus*, is the most copious
"on this head, and therein he speaks plain-
"ly of ' one sempiternal and unoriginated
"God; which God, says *Plato*, when he
"reasoned within himself about a future
"God, made this universe, and placed this
"perfectly happy God which he begat, as
"the *soul in the middle of it*ᵈ." The words
sempiternal and *unoriginated* have a pompous sound; but as we are certain that these philosophers dignified the first matter of the universe with these attributes, they are nothing but mere sounds without either sense or meaning; for whatever noise they make with the attributes of *eternity*, *wisdom*, *goodness*, *perfection*, and the like; yet, if they bestowed these high appellations upon a wrong object, upon that which *by nature is not God*, the most subtile reasonings in the world cannot clear them from the odious imputation of having dishonoured that God, whom we are told, *they did not like to retain in their knowledge*ᵉ. All that can be done (or at least all that I have seen) upon this occasion, is to presume that

ᵈ Το ον αιι, γενεσιν δε ουκ εχον.   ᵉ P. 127.   ᶠ Rom. i. 28.

that the wife Heathens could not be so *absurd* as to overlook the power of a Creator, and ascribe divine intelligence to the dead elements of the world. But this can amount to little or nothing; because, whether they were so absurd or not, is the very question in dispute, and nothing but their own expressions, compared with the character they bear in the sacred writings, ought to decide it.

But let us descend to a closer examination of *Plato's* words. This *sempiternal* and *unoriginated* God, it seems, when he *reasoned within himself about a future God, made this universe*. The formation of the universe, therefore, was necessary to the existence of this *future God*. If to this his residence be added, it must, I apprehend, at once dispel all farther doubts and difficulties. For when he was begotten, he was placed in this universe, as the *soul in the middle* of it. Now what is it that is placed in the *middle* of the universe, but the *light* in the orb of the *sun*, the first and chief of all the *forms* that emerged from the obscurity of primæval darkness? This is the

soul

soul *Plato* speaks of, and accordingly it is confessed by *Heraiscus* in *Damascius*, that the *sun*, here called the *soul in the middle*, is the νες νοητος, the *intelligent mind* of the world[r]. So that this *perfectly happy God* is, after all, nothing greater than the *Egyptian Cneph, begotten out of sand and water.* This is sufficient to give us a surfeit of *Plato*'s Trinity, and, therefore, any farther account of it would be superfluous. But the *Essay-writer* thinks it " more for " his purpose" to take this Trinity as delivered by *Porphyry*, " who flourished about " the time when the *consubstantial* doctrine " of the Trinity began (as he calls it) to " *make a noise*[s]:" Which observation, though improperly worded, is yet in the main true enough; so true, that it will at once overturn all he has attempted to build upon it. This *Porphyry* was an apostate from the *Christian* to the *Heathen* religion, and opposed the gospel with the most implacable bitterness, even to a degree of madness: this principle encouraged him to draw up the opinion of *Plato* in the very terms

[r] Bp. Cumb. *Ibid.* p. 282.   [s] P. 130.

terms made ufe of by the primitive Fathers to exprefs the doctrine of the *facred Trinity*; and in fo doing his intent was, impudently to confront the *Chriftians* with this contemptible fcrap of Paganifm, dreffed up in their own expreffions. The words of *Porphyry* are thefe—Αχρι γαρ τριων υποϛασεων, εφη Πλατων, την τȣ Θεȣ προελθειν ȣσιαν, &c. "Plato *faid, that the* effence *of God is diftinguifhed into three* Hypoftafes," &c. *Plato* never faid any fuch thing; he never thought of defining his confufed triplicity by the terms ȣσια and υποϛασις properly applied and diftinguifhed: and when ornamented with this garb, it makes, I think, a much worfe appearance than it did before. So that *Porphyry*, by his fenfe of the *Platonic* Trinity, inftead of betraying the weaknefs of the confubftantial doctrine, betrays nothing but his own want of judgment. He has borrowed the moft diftinguifhed terms from the Chriftians of his time, and by an injudicious application of them, made that Trinity a confubftantial one, which according to its original and genuine acceptation, was never defigned as fuch. Upon

Upon the whole then, there will be no danger in granting, that "it is manifeſt (as "our author aſſerts) beyond all controverſy, "that both *Plato* and his diſciples held a "kind of eſſential ſubordination to have "exiſted between theſe Gods[b];" for the argument drawn from a compariſon between an heathen and the ſcriptural Trinity is ſo inconſequential, that if he had inſtanced a ſubordination in fifty more Trinities of the like nature, it would not in the leaſt effect the ſenſe of this doctrine as maintained by believers.

I ſhall, therefore, purſue this ſubject no farther, and ought to beg the reader's pardon, for dwelling ſo long upon ſo dry a ſubject; but as it was preſſed into the ſervice of heterodoxy, I thought it could not be amiſs to ſet this matter in that light, in which the Pagans themſelves appear to have ſeen it. Some modern critics by putting a more ſublime ſenſe upon theſe things, have contradicted the original deſign of them, and diſplayed their own ignorance in a very pompous manner: they have exalted the pro-

[b] P. 132.

prophane abfurdities of heathenifm, while they have made no fcruple of depreciating the myfteries of true religion. They have been fo hardy as to apprehend without the leaft ceremony that when the ancient philofophers fpeak of their Gods and Dæmons, they muft mean the fame as a believer does by the true God, and the hoft of angels. This is a fact too well known to need any particular proof; but, however, I fhall produce one inftance of it from the great *Bochart*, which, as this learned man was not lefs fkilled in facred than in prophane knowledge, is fo much the more remarkable, and may ferve to teach us, that before we venture to affert an agreement between the Bible and the heathen cofmogonies in any article of moment, fome caution is abfolutely neceffary.

Sanchoniatho, in his cofmogony, after he has afferted his firft dark principle of the univerfe, and a fecond God begotten of him by a felf-concupifcence, fets down, in the third order, a fort of dæmons or intelligent animals, which he calls *Zophefemin*, fpies or infpectors of the heavens, each of them

them formed in the fhape of an egg, and generated from mud[i]; which *Zophefemin* are fuppofed by *Bochart*, to mean the celeftial angels, the intelligent and real inhabitants of the invifible heavens. A criticifm fo evidently abfurd and contrary to truth, that I fhall not undertake to difprove it; and the rather, becaufe it is taken proper notice of by the learned bifhop *Cumberland*[k].

This unaccountable fancy of fearching for facred truth amongft the writings of profeffed idolaters, hath had too many and too

[i] Eufeb. Præp. Evan. lib. i. c. 10.

[k] The learned *Bochart* hath rightly given the original of the name *Zophefemim* from the *Hebrew* צפה, fignifying *fpeculators* or *obfervers*, and שמים *heaven*; but he does violence to the author's whole text and fcope; befides that he oppofes *Eufebius*'s juft reflection upon him, as not propounding the inhabitants of heaven, *i. e.* the angels, for Deities, when he interprets thefe *Zophefemim* to be angels. For how fhould angels be bred, as thefe are faid to be, out of mud? How, when angels are fo generated, fhall the fun, moon, and ftars, fhine out? how fhall angels be fhaped like an egg, or in a roundifh form? The truth is, his mind was prepoffeffed with Chriftian notions, and he vainly imagined that an Heathen muft be fo too. But *Sanchoniatho* meant only, that the celeftial bodies are *intelligent*, and fee what is done here below; and, therefore, were to be adored as Gods. *Remark: upon the Hift. of Sanch.* p. 21.

too able advocates both ancient and modern; and though we ought not to fuspect, that in all cafes it proceeds from a very bad principle, yet can it feldom or never be referred to a very good one; and the attempt muſt be in general fruitleſs and unfatisfactory: for though it be granted, that upon the rife and progreſs of idolatry after the flood, the moſt ancient Heathens carried off many fublime myſteries of the true religion, and purloined more in after ages from the people of God; yet when they were in poffeffion of them, they mixed them up with their own atheiſtical principles, then ſtrained away the purer part of the mixture, and let it run to waſte: fo that if we now feek it again from them, there is little to be found but their own filthy fediments inſtead of it. And if in fcattered fragments, borrowed from the *Hebrews*, there fhould be found fome dark notices of the true God, yet, after all, we are not to form our fentiments from the Heathen theology, but to reform and correct that by the Chriſtian.

CHAP.

CHAP. VIII.

His remarks upon the Athanasian *and* Nicene *Creeds obviated.*

THE intent of the essay-writer in these remarks is, to point out a few contradictions both in the language and in the sense of these two Creeds, when compared either with themselves, or with each other. But, I fear, that whatever contradictions we shall meet with, they will at last prove to be nothing but the genuine produce of his own imagination. I will try the experiment, by setting down these remarks separately, and subjoining a reply to each of them.

Remark I. " The doctrine of *three Hy-*
" *postases,* was not the doctrine of the
" council of *Nice,* but was afterwards a-
" dopted by some of the *Consubstantialists,*
" and was inserted in that Creed which
" goes under the name of *Athanasius;* but
" which could not possibly have been writ-
" ten by him, because he, as well as the
" rest

"rest of the *Nicene* Fathers, insisted upon
"it, that there was but *one Hypostasis* in
"the Trinity, any more than one *Usia*[1].

His reason then for affirming that the Creed which goes under the name of *Athanasius*, could not *possibly* have been written by him, is, because he *insisted upon it*, that there was but *one Hypostasis* in the Trinity, any more than one *Usia*. This cannot possibly be true, because on the contrary *Athanasius insisted upon it*, that in the Trinity, there is one *Usia* and *three Hypostases*: as a proof of which, the following instances will be esteemed sufficient. In his *Questions* *, we find these two, with their respective answers—*How many* Essences *do you confess in the Godhead?* Ans. *I confess* ONE Essence, *one Nature*, &c. Qu. *How many* Hypostases *do you confess in the Godhead?* Ans. *I confess* THREE HYPOSTASES

or

---

[1] P. 135.

* The author himself having cited these *Questions* of *Athanasius*, can have no right to object to their authority. However, to satisfy all scruples, let the reader consult that undoubtedly genuine oration, *Unum esse Christum*, in which *hypostasis* and *prosupon* are used throughout as equivalent terms.

or *Persons* [m], &c. And again, in his *Dialogue* with a *Macedonian*, he says, Τεως εμαθες οτι και η παλαια Διαθηκη οιδεν τας ΤΡΕΙΣ Υποςασεις [n]. *Hitherto you have been made to understand, that even the Old Testament declares for the doctrine of* THREE *Hypostases.* It is likewise clear, that *Athanasius* never meant to confound the sense of these terms, so as to make them synonymous, because he has explained the one *Hypostasis*, by προσωπον, *person*, and the other, *Usia*, by φυσις, *nature*; which are as distinct in their significations, as any other terms whatever. That the term *Hypostasis* as applied to the *personality*, is not of later date than the *Nicene* age, appears even from an epistle of *Arius* himself preserved by *Epiphanius*, and written to *Alexander* bishop of *Alexandria* before the *Nicene* council. We therein observe the following words—Ωςε τρεις εισιν υποςασεις, πατηρ, Υιος, και Αγιον Πνευμα. vid. Epiph. Hæres. LXIX.

II.

---

[m] Επι τε θεε ποσας εσιας ομολογεις; ΑΠ. Μιαν εσιαν λεγω, μιαν φυσιν, &c. ΕΡ. Υποςασεις δε ποσας ομολογεις επι τε θεε; ΑΠ. Τρεις υποςασεις ομολογω, τρια προσωπα, &c. V. II. p. 442.

[n] V. I. p. 223.

II. "*Socrates*, the ecclefiaftical hiftorian "fays from *Iræneus*" (the *grammarian*, not the *Father)* " that though the word *Hypo-* "*ftafis* was not ufed by the more ancient " philofophers, yet, fays he, you muft un- " derftand that the moderns make ufe of " it inftead of ઠσια°."

Socrates does not fpeak of the *moderns*, as intimating the *Chriftians*, but the modern *Greek* philofophers; and our bufinefs at prefent is not with them, but with the intention of the *Nicene* Fathers.

III. " To fay therefore that the three " Perfons in the Trinity are one *Ufia* and " three *Hypoftafes*, is the fame thing as to " fay, that they are *one fubftance* and *three* " *fubftances* at the fame time; which I take " to be a contradiction in terms, and there- " fore cannot be affirmed even of God " himfelfᵖ."

No: it is the fame thing as to fay, that they are *three perfons* and *one nature*; fince *Athanafius* explains the word *Hypoftafis* by προσωπον, *perfon*, and *Ufia* by φυσις, *nature*; which is therefore fo far from being a contradiction

° P. 136.   ᵖ Ibid. and 137.

contradiction in terms, that it is the very thing the church means to exprefs and infift upon.

IV. "When it is faid in the *Nicene* Creed, that the Son is εκ της ȣσιας τȣ Πατρος, *of the fubftance of the Father*, and that he is ομοȣσιℨ τω Πατρι, *of one fubftance with the Father*—wherein does the difference confift? Why, in being faid to be *three* fubftances at the fame time that they are but *one* fubftance[q]."

It is not faid, either in this place or any where elfe, that the Perfons of the Trinity are *three fubftances*; but when a man is fo violently heated with his own opinion, he makes but a very indifferent critic. By the former of thefe expreffions, we are to underftand (as it is faid in the Creed itfelf) that the Son was γεννηθεντα, *begotten*, εκ της ȣσιας, *of* or *from the fubftance* of the Father, and by the latter, that when fo begotten, he was ομοȣσιℨ, of the *fame fubftance* nature, or effence, with the Father, though a different *Perfon* from him. If he was begotten of the Father, he muft be of the same

[q] Ibid.

fame effence or nature from which he was begotten, and yet is not to be confounded in perfon with the Father: which was the herefy of *Sabellius,* who maintained that the Trinity was μονοπροσωπ⊙, *i. e.* that it confifted of one Perfon numerically the fame, but τριωνυμ⊙, diftinguifhed by three different appellations.

V. " I am very fenfible that in our *En-*
" *glifh* tranflation of the Creed, commonly
" called the *Athanafian* Creed, we have
" followed the church of *Rome,* whofe in-
" fallibility can give what fenfe it pleafes
" to words, in rendering the word Υποςασις
" by the *Englifh* word *perfon,* that church
" having rendered it by the *Latin* word
" *perfona*'."

Athanafius, Epiphanius, and all the *Greek* Fathers', have expounded it by the *Greek* word προσωπον, *perfon;* and therefore we have not followed the church of *Rome's Latin*

' P. 138.

* Υποςασις και προσωπον ταυτον ιςι παρ' αυτοις. *Hypoftafis & perfona idem eft apud illos.* Sc. Patres. Leont. De Sect. p. 388. And *Suidas* affirms, that Υποςασις κατα την εκκλησιαςικην και αποςολικην παραδοσιν ιςι τω προσωπον—*Hypoftafis,* according to ecclefiaftical and apoftolical tradition, is the fame with *perfon.*

Latin word. This remark is succeeded by a long and moſt perplexed criticiſm upon the different acceptations of the word *perſon*, as applied to *men:* which is all wide of the purpoſe; becauſe we have no concern either with its application to diſtinct and ſeparate men, or to the ſame man conſidered in different capacities, but to the Godhead: and when thus applied, we know what we would mean by it, and ſcorn any low equivocations about it. This attempt upon the *words* whereby we expreſs our faith, is no new thing; for whoever is in the leaſt converſant with eccleſiaſtical antiquity, will find that the *Arians* always harboured the moſt implacable enmity againſt them: for which, no other cauſe can be aſſigned, than that theſe terms, when applied ſo properly as they are in the Creeds, cut their hereſy up by the roots—*hinc illæ lachrymæ!* But their wrath did not confine itſelf to the terms; did likewiſe moſt amply exert itſelf againſt the *Nicene* Biſhops, who, with others that embraced their ſentiments, were reported by the *Arian* fraternity to be no better than *fools* and *idiots*[e], while themſelves

[e] See *Socr. Schol.* lib. i. ch. 9.

selves were the only wife and knowing amongst mankind.

VI. " I cannot help saying, it is some-
" thing odd to have these two Creeds (the
" *Nicene* and *Athanasian*) established in the
" same church, in one of which those are
" declared to be accursed, who deny the
" Son to be of the same *Hypostasis* or *Usia*
" with the Father; and in the other, it is
" declared *they cannot be saved*, who do not
" assert, that *there is one Hypostasis of the*
" *Father, and another of the Son, and an-*
" *other of the Holy Ghost*[u]."

This seeming contradiction arises only from his confounding the words ουσια and υποϛασις: for though it be said, in the *anathema* annexed at the end of the *Nicene* Creed, that they are accursed who say that the Son is *of any other Hypostasis* or *Usia* than of the Father, yet when it is considered, that the Son is of the *Hypostasis* in one sense, and of the *Usia* in another, the *Athanasian* and *Nicene* Creeds are not at variance. Thus, the Son, as *God*, is *of* the Father's *Usia*, and partakes of that divine

nature

[u] P. 146.

nature or *essence*, from which he is generated: as a *Son*, he is begotten of the Father's *Hypostasis* or *Person*; which makes the contradiction vanish entirely; since it shews, that there may be three *Hypostases* in the Godhead, as the *Athanasian* Creed sets forth; and that the Son may be begotten of the Father's *Hypostasis*, as it is asserted in the *Nicene*. But, even supposing his observation upon this *anathema* to be just, yet his suspicion of *oddness* in the establishment of the church is altogether groundless; since it is wholly omitted in that form of the *Nicene* Creed inserted in our *Book of Common Prayer*; and therefore it is weak to calumniate the Protestant church, for establishing what it hath never established at all.

These are all the remarks I thought it necessary to take any notice of. But the author of them, supposing they have put us into such disorder, that our only way is, to make a fair retreat, and give up the matter as unintelligible, bestows upon us the following sneer—" In order to obviate all
" these objections, it is thought sufficient

"by some, to say, that there are many
"powers in the divine nature, which hu-
"man beings are not capable of compre-
"hending*." But, with humble submission, we are not reduced to this method of
obviating these objections: and though such
a declamatory method would have spared
me much trouble, yet have I endeavoured
to set these objections aside, by shewing
that, in effect, there are no real objections
either against the sense of a Trinity in
Unity, or against the manner in which this
doctrine is set forth in the Creeds. For
whatever degree of humility and acqui-
escence is expected in relation to the articles
of our faith, neither the scripture, nor the
church-catholic requires us to believe that
the Holy Trinity are one and three in *one
and the same respect*; which would indeed
be a most insuperable contradiction: but
in the sense we hold it, there is no contradiction at all.

As for his frequent use of the name *Consubstantialists*, as if those, who believe a
consubstantial Trinity, were some private
                                        party

*P. 146.

party or sect of christians dissenting from the truth—his charging us with following the *Pope's infallibility*—and his affirming with such confidence, that the *revelation of this wonderful doctrine came originally from the Papal chair*[x]—in all this he is as equitable as when he compares us to the *bigoted members of the Church of Rome*, for shewing some regard to sincerity and moral honesty in our subscription to Creeds and Articles. For though in the holy scriptures it be not asserted *totidem literis*, that the Trinity is *consubstantial*, yet is it expressly declared, that *the Lord our God is* ONE JEHOVAH, and that *the Father, Son, and Holy Ghost, are* ONE, that is, one eternal nature, co-equal in majesty, wisdom, power, and every other attribute of essential divinity. At our baptism we are, after the ordinance of *Christ* our Lord, solemnly initiated into the faith of a Trinity in Unity— The inspired Apostles, and from them the church-catholic, pronounce their blessings in strict conformity with this faith, as the High Priest, on the day of the great yearly atonement, did upon the *Israelites* by a three-

[x] P. 151.

threefold repetition of the name *Jehovah*[y]: and the two Testaments, as hath been shewn, abound with the revelation of this divine mystery.

It is therefore, without all controversy, a scriptural truth, that the Godhead is ONE, and that in this Godhead there are *Three Persons:* and if the *author* can devise any method of expressing their *unity* more fully and more sensibly than by the word *consubstantial*, let him advance it: but to represent the whole as of no higher an original than the *Papal chair*, when even the very word *consubstantial* was not borrowed from thence, is to betray the weakness of his own cause, and offer an affront to the common sense of every *Protestant* Christian.

Another method he takes of blending this doctrine and Popery together, is by observing, that " when the *Protestants* ar-
" gue against the doctrine of *transubstanti-*
" *ation*, the *Papists* never fail objecting
" the equal incredibility of a *consubstantial*
" Trinity[z]." This is very true: but a *Protestant* is not bound to answer for the indiscretion of a *Papist*, in putting the doctrine

[y] Numb. vi. 24.   [z] Ibid.

trine of a *confubstantial* Trinity upon a level with a *tranfubstantiation* of the facramental elements: and a parallel between thefe two doctrines cannot poffibly turn out to the difadvantage of the former, fince the one is fubjected to the fcrutiny of our fenfes, and contradicts them; the other is above our fenfes, and does not contradict our reafon. If indeed he rejects the myftery of a Trinity in Unity, becaufe he is pleafed to think it *incredible*, the argument drawn from hence carries with it no more weight than that of a bad example; the ill effect of which is always rendered as extenfive as poffible by others of the fame perfuafion; who take infinite pains by the means of News Papers and Reviews to deceive the ignorant, and make the Coffee-houfes ring with the praifes of fuch *reformed Theology* as that of this *Effay*, and other weaker writtings upon the fame fubject; that we may become *ripe for reformation*, that is, ready to abjure the primitive faith, and to receive in its ftead either the fcepticifm of *Bayle*, or the enthufiaftic philofophy of *Socinus*. The chriftian reader, I truft, will not take me for his enemy if I give him warning

not

not to be imposed upon by such reports, but to *prove all things and hold fast that which is good*. The question is not, whether a Trinity was believed by *Hoadley*, *Clarke*, or *Clayton*; but whether it is revealed in the Holy Scripture, not a syllable of which will be invalidated by the disbelief of the whole world. For every controversy concerning the mysteries of our religion will have a second and a more solemn hearing; when God who gave the Word shall come to make inquisition how it hath been received and followed. Our *Arians* therefore will do well to consider, not how they may put a face upon their cause in the sight of men, by misrepresenting the scripture, depreciating the primitive Fathers and Martyrs, applauding to the skies every deistical scribbler, scoffing at uniformity, railing at orthodoxy, and publishing all manner of scandal against the church and the friends of it; but how all their pretended reformations will appear in the sight of God; before whom they must either maintain them as they do now, or take the consequences; for it will be too late to retract!

F I N I S.

www.ingramcontent.com/pod-product-compliance
Lightning Source LLC
Chambersburg PA
CBHW032132230426
43672CB00011B/2310